TOTALLY RANDOM QUESTIONS

QUESTIONS

VOLUME 7

101 Wondrous and Wacky Q&As

Melina Gerosa Bellows

BRIGHT MATTER BOOKS

New York

Contents

Where did the world's largest snowball fight break out? **9**

True or False: Elephants can jump. **11**

How often does the International Space Station circle Earth? **13**

Where is the Disgusting Food Museum located? **15**

True or False: Ancient humans couldn't drink cow's milk. **17**

When is the brain most active? **19**

True or False: Praying mantids see in 3-D. **21**

True or False: Cats are afraid of cucumbers. **23**

Which city has the world's largest population? **25**

What is the Vomit Comet? **27**

Where did the salt in your kitchen originally come from? **29**

True or False: Hummingbirds are color-blind. **31**

What is the largest island on Earth? **33**

True or False: Some spiders eat their webs. **35**

True or False: Bones are the only human body parts that don't contain water. **37**

What is the most remote place on Earth? **39**

How many days does the Tour de France last? **41**

How many grooves are on a U.S. quarter? **43**

True or False: All puppies are born deaf. **45**

How many ribs do most humans have? **47**

True or False: Liquids can't form puddles in space. **49**

What is cryotherapy? **51**

Why do cats stop eating before their bowls are empty? **53**

True or False: Pinecones can predict the weather. **55**

True or False: A dolphin's skin is thicker than an elephant's. **57**

Why is Africa known as the Cradle of Humankind? **59**

Which country has the most pet dogs? **61**

True or False: Llamas are helping scientists research ways to treat COVID-19. **63**

The Cuvier's beaked whale can hold its breath for how many hours? **65**

Which site is one of the New Seven Wonders of the World? **67**

What gives saltwater crocodiles their deadly bite? **69**

True or False: Mars makes a humming noise. **71**

Which country has built the most cars? **73**

How many muscles does it take to smile? **75**

True or False: Spittlebugs live in a home that's made with their own pee. **77**

What is the world's longest mountain range? **79**

How do small tugboats pull huge ships? **81**

Which rodent lives the longest? **83**

True or False: Human activity can affect clouds. **85**

Which internal organ can regrow? **87**

True or False: Sharks don't have bones. **89**

What is the closest major galaxy to the Milky Way? **91**

How many vocal cords do cats have? **93**

True or False: Beavers were once the size of bears. **95**

How fast can the world's current fastest human run? **97**

Which part of a pigeon weighs the most? **99**

True or False: Doing good deeds can make you happy. **101**

True or False: A metal can be a gas. **103**

How many miles of blood vessels are in the human body? **105**

What was *Meganeuropsis*? **107**

True or False: Oysters can change their gender. **109**

How many sides does a snowflake have? **111**

What does the word *astronaut* loosely mean in Greek? **113**

True or False: A stadium full of fans can improve an athlete's performance. **115**

True or False: Dogs stick their heads out of car windows to smell their surroundings. **117**

How big was the largest hailstone ever recorded? **119**

True or False: Dolphins don't live in Arctic or Antarctic waters. **121**

What was Ada Lovelace known for? **123**

True or False: Your skull's bones don't move. **125**

How did glass frogs get their name? **127**

True or False: Yodeling can cause an avalanche. **129**

Why do you often see rocks around train tracks? **131**

True or False: Racecar drivers are considered athletes. **133**

Who patented the telephone? **135**

How big are the eyes of a giant squid? **137**

Why do dogs kick backward after they go to the bathroom? **139**

True or False: A place must have at least 10 residents to qualify as a "town." **141**

Which sense is most closely connected to memory? **143**

Why do turtles have shells? **145**

True or False: Playing is good for your brain. **147**

Which primate is most closely related to chimpanzees? **149**

True or False: Water always boils at the same temperature. **151**

How many hairs are on the average human head? **153**

What is the deepest lake on Earth? **155**

Who invented the cotton candy machine? **157**

What do cardinals sometimes put all over their bodies? **159**

True or False: Fish cough. **161**

How are medicines made? **163**

According to scientists, why do people participate in dangerous sports? **165**

How many flowers must honeybees visit to produce a pound (0.5 kg) of honey? **167**

When the *Titanic* sank in 1912, how many dogs survived? **169**

True or False: Tigers have striped skin. **171**

What's the most complex organ in the body? **173**

What has been banned from Antarctica? **175**

True or False: Only female animals give birth. **177**

Why do professional swimmers and cyclists sometimes shave their legs? **179**

Who invented meteorology? **181**

True or False: Cats sweat. **183**

What is a large raindrop shaped like? **185**

True or False: Alligators prey on manatees. **187**

What is heterochromia? **189**

Why do wildebeests migrate? **191**

True or False: You can walk to Russia from the United States. **193**

How much food can an adult's stomach hold? **195**

Which of these was true about Coco Chanel? **197**

How long is one year on Uranus? **199**

What happens to your hair strands as you age? **201**

How do pigs protect their skin from the sun? **203**

True or False: Human teeth are as strong as shark teeth. **205**

What does a black hole do to a passing star? **207**

A dog's nose is about how many times more sensitive than a human's nose? **209**

Spot the Difference **211**

Index **212**

Photo Credits **214**

Credits **215**

Where did the world's largest snowball fight break out?

a. Sweden

b. South Korea

c. Canada

Japanese macaque

NOW YOU KNOW!
Monkeys called Japanese macaques have been known to create balls of snow and smash them into each other's faces. They have even been observed stealing snowballs and chasing each other to get them back.

ANSWER: c Canada

THE WORLD'S LARGEST SNOWBALL FIGHT INCLUDED 7,681 PEOPLE AND TOOK PLACE IN SASKATOON, CANADA. The event, held in 2016, was part of a farewell send-off for Canada's professional snowball fighting team, held before they headed to Japan for a world championship match! The team was one of more than 100 teams that travel to the Showa-Shinzan International Yukigassen competition each year. In the sport of yukigassen, which means "snow battle" in Japanese, teams face off in a game that's part dodgeball, part capture the flag—and 100 percent cool!

CANADA
SASKATOON
SASKATCHEWAN

Instant Genius
The fear of snow is called "chionophobia."

Kangaroo rat

ANSWER: False

JUMPING REQUIRES STRONG LEG MUSCLES AND FLEXIBLE ANKLES, AND ELEPHANTS HAVE NEITHER. Even if they did, these massive animals are simply too heavy to lift themselves off the ground. **Animals tend to jump to escape danger and defend themselves against predators.** Elephants instead rely on their size and strength to defend themselves against most threats. **Rhinos and hippos can't jump either, but they can sometimes lift all four feet off the ground while running.** Scientists aren't totally sure if elephants actually run, because all four feet never leave the ground—but they do appear to bounce when moving at higher speeds!

How often does the International
Space Station
circle Earth?

a. **every 90 minutes**

b. **every 9 days**

c. **every 90 days**

13

International Space Station cupola

NOW YOU KNOW!
On board the ISS, there are two bathrooms, a gym, six sleeping compartments, and a 360-degree bay window to take in the spectacular galactic view.

Instant Genius
It takes 8 miles (13 km) of wire to connect the electrical system of the ISS.

ANSWER: a   every 90 minutes

THE INTERNATIONAL SPACE STATION (ISS) CIRCLES EARTH EVERY 90 MINUTES. It travels around 17,500 miles (28,164 km) an hour. In one day, the ISS travels the distance to the moon and back! In the night sky, the ISS is as bright as the planet Venus. You can see it in the sky without a telescope if you know where to look. **The International Space Station got its name because many countries collaborated to create it.** Altogether, 249 people from 19 countries have stayed on the ISS. **There are normally seven astronauts on the ISS at a time.** They spend most of their days keeping the spaceship in good shape, doing experiments, and exploring places like the moon and Mars.

INTERNATIONAL SPACE STATION

Where is the **Disgusting Food Museum** located?

a. **Netherlands**

b. **Sweden**

INTERNET

c. **on the internet**

#4

15

The Disgusting Food Museum, Sweden

ANSWER: b Sweden

THE DISGUSTING FOOD MUSEUM IS IN SWEDEN AND HAS MORE THAN 80 DIFFERENT FOODS FROM ALL AROUND THE GLOBE THAT HAVE BEEN DEEMED "DISGUSTING." The ticket to enter also acts as a barf bag—just in case you need it during your visit. Some of the foods featured include fermented shark meat and cooked guinea pig. **Some American foods like Twinkies and root beer are there because they are unappealing to many people outside the United States. Psychologist Samuel West, the man who created this bizarre museum, wanted to challenge what audiences perceive as disgusting.** Although one person might find something really gross, others might genuinely like it. West also created the Museum of Failure, which has exhibits in other places, like Shanghai, China, and California, U.S.A. Some of the Museum of Failure exhibits include green ketchup and a perfume that smells like motorcycles.

5

True or False:

ncient humans couldn't drink

cow's milk.

NOW YOU KNOW!

Only 35 percent of people can digest lactose, which means that their bodies can break down milk products into sugars that the body can absorb and turn into energy.

ANSWER: **True**

HUMANS WERE CONSUMING DAIRY PRODUCTS IN SOME FORM AT LEAST 6,500 YEARS AGO. But back then, the human body did not have a way to digest plain cow's milk—until humans learned to ferment it. In fermentation, sugars—such as the lactose in milk—are broken down and used up. This makes the milk easier to digest. The fermented milk, which took the form of cheese and curds, had more nutrients and was easier to keep, too. Over thousands of years, the human body has slowly adapted and the gene to digest milk has become more common in the larger population, though even today many people still can't digest the stuff.

Instant Genius

Milk gets its white color from the fat inside it.

When is the brain most active?

#6

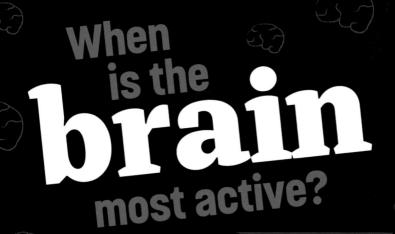

b. when you sleep

a. when you read

c. when you run

Instant Genius

People spend about one-third of their lives sleeping on average.

ANSWER: b when you sleep

YOUR BRAIN DOES NOT "TURN OFF" WHEN YOU SLEEP. Some parts of your brain actually turn on when you catch some shut-eye! **As you sleep, the nerve cells in your brain work hard to digest new information you learned that day and to refresh themselves for the day ahead.** Your brain reaches its most active state when you're dreaming. **Those vivid, almost-felt-real dreams happen during the deepest stage of sleep, called REM sleep.** REM stands for rapid eye movement, which happens as you encounter new images in a dream. **Because your brain is making so many new connections at this time, sleeping often boosts creativity and helps people come up with ideas.**

True or False:

Praying mantids
see in 3-D.

#7

21

NOW YOU KNOW!

Praying mantids get their name from the shape of their long front legs with spiky claws on the tips. With these, mantids can quickly grab and hold prey, such as grasshoppers, moths, crickets, and even hummingbirds!

ANSWER: True

Instant Genius

Praying mantids have long necks and can turn their heads 180 degrees.

PRAYING MANTIDS ARE THE ONLY INVERTEBRATES WITH THE UNIQUE ABILITY OF SEEING THINGS IN 3-D, SORT OF LIKE LOOKING THROUGH A PAIR OF BUILT-IN BINOCULARS—A KIND OF VISION KNOWN AS STEREOPSIS. Equipped with eyes both in the middle and on the sides of their heads, the insects can detect even the slightest movements of their prey. **The coloring of the praying mantid—which lives mostly in tropical areas—allows its body to blend in with its surroundings, so the mantid can go undetected.** Scientists are studying the incredible eyes of these insects to develop vision for robots.

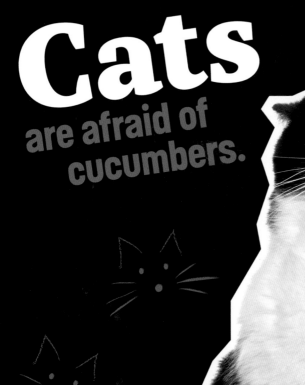

True or False:

Cats
are afraid of
cucumbers.

ANSWER: True

CUCUMBERS LOOK LIKE SNAKES—AT LEAST TO CATS. And cats are very afraid of snakes! Felines are extremely alert and attuned to their surroundings, so seeing something new can be startling. **An unexpected encounter with a cucumber can cause an immediate reaction for a cat.** It may jump several feet in the air, just like a human reacting to, well, a snake on the kitchen floor. This is the cat's instincts. **In the wild, cats have learned to avoid snakes because they're dangerous.** Domestic cats can conquer this fear by being exposed to more cucumbers. Eventually the cat would get used to the shape and learn it doesn't actually slither or bite. However, vets warn against trying this on your own. Pranking your cat may cause it to develop severe stress and anxiety.

Python

Which city has the world's largest population?

b. Tokyo, Japan

a. New York City, U.S.A.

c. London, United Kingdom

Shibuya Crossing, Tokyo, Japan

NOW YOU KNOW!

The cherry blossom, from flowering cherry trees, is the national symbol of Japan. In 1912, Japan gifted the United States with 3,000 of the trees.

ANSWER: b Tokyo, Japan

IN 2021, TOKYO HAD AN ESTIMATED 13.96 MILLION PEOPLE. **The Tokyo metropolitan area, which includes less-populated surrounding areas, has more than 37 million people in total.** These surrounding areas share an economy and industry with the city. **Despite the huge amount of people, Tokyo has low unemployment and crime rates.** Traffic moves quickly here, and people have access to many forms of transportation, such as trains, subways, and inexpensive bikes. Tokyo's Shibuya Crossing is the busiest pedestrian crossing in the world. Up to 3,000 people coming from all different directions cross at a time, **earning it the nickname "The Scramble."**

What is the
Vomit Comet?

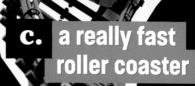

b. a vehicle that mimics conditions in space

c. a really fast roller coaster

a. a gigantic ice cream cone

The crew of STS-44 mission undergoing zero-gravity training

HANKS   BACON   PAXTON   SINISE   HARRIS

APOLLO 13

ANSWER: b **a vehicle that mimics space**

THINK OF A ROLLER COASTER IN THE SKY, ON AN AIRPLANE. It would be a lot like the Vomit Comet, a high-tech airplane that flies over the Gulf of Mexico and was designed to simulate weightlessness. Why would anyone want to do this? Well, it helps astronauts get used to being in microgravity, which is what astronauts experience in space. **It's called the Vomit Comet because all that motion makes astronauts in training very nauseous—on purpose.** Just like a roller coaster, the Vomit Comet goes up a steep incline and then has a period of weightlessness before the big drop. Then it zooms back down toward Earth with twice the force of gravity. **NASA has retired the aircraft, but a private company still offers rides.**

Instant Genius

Scenes for the space movie *Apollo 13* were filmed on the Vomit Comet.

Where did the **salt** in your kitchen originally come from?

#11

a. the solar system

b. the ocean

c. Earth's crust

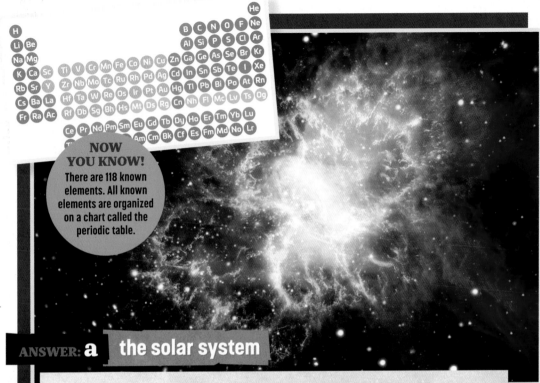

ANSWER: a the solar system

MANY OF EARTH'S ELEMENTS, INCLUDING THE SALT IN YOUR KITCHEN, COME FROM THE SOLAR SYSTEM. An element is a substance that cannot be split into simpler substances through ordinary chemical reactions. Most elements are metals, such as gold, aluminum, and mercury. **The three lightest elements—hydrogen, helium, and a small amount of lithium—appeared after the big bang, when particles in space started smashing together.** About 500 million years later, those elements turned into stars, which exploded to form more elements. **Every time a star dies, it leaves behind a huge number of elementary particles.** These elements float around in space until they find a place where a new star is being formed. **They then become part of the new stars. This is how the sun was created.** Then leftover, floating elements clumped together to make the rest of the planets, including Earth.

Hummingbirds
are color-blind.

#12

NOW YOU KNOW!
Scientists believe that, just like hummingbirds, dinosaurs were probably tetrachromatic. Some fish and reptiles are, too.

ANSWER: **False**

HUMMINGBIRDS CAN SEE MORE COLORS THAN HUMANS CAN! Both birds and humans detect color from a part of the eye called cones. Humans are trichromatic, meaning we have three cones that detect blue, green, and red light, allowing us to see all the colors of the rainbow. **Hummingbirds also have a fourth cone that is sensitive to ultraviolet light, which makes them tetrachromatic.** This gives them the ability to see colors we can't even imagine. This unique color-spotting ability helps them find food, pick mates, and avoid predators. **Humans never evolved this seeing superpower because our survival didn't depend on distinguishing between daylight colors. Instead, humans (who are mammals) figured out how to survive by prowling at night.**

What is the largest island on Earth?

c. Borneo

a. Greenland

b. Great Britain

Instant Genius

Greenland is the largest island in the world that is not a continent.

Colorful homes in Greenland

ANSWER: a Greenland

NOW YOU KNOW!
Greenland is part of the country of Denmark. It's inhabited mostly by Inuit people.

AN ISLAND IS A LANDMASS SURROUNDED COMPLETELY BY WATER. Five of the world's islands are very big, covering an area of more than 190,000 square miles (492,100 sq km). **These islands are Baffin in Canada, Madagascar off the east coast of Africa, Borneo in Asia, New Guinea north of Australia, and—the biggest—Greenland.** Icy and cold, Greenland spans 840,000 square miles (2,175,590 sq km). Two-thirds of the island sits inside the Arctic Circle. Global warming is posing a problem for Greenland because the massive ice sheet that covers most of the island is melting. **This affects not only the people, but also the animals that live there—including polar bears, arctic foxes, lemmings, and snow hares.**

34

True or False:

Some spiders eat their webs.

#14

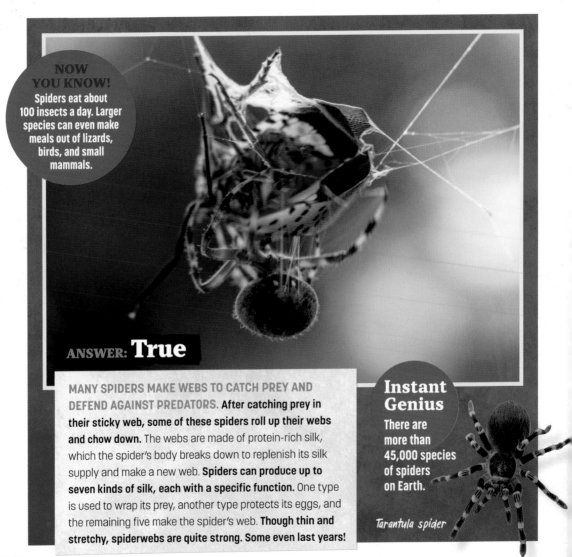

NOW YOU KNOW!

Spiders eat about 100 insects a day. Larger species can even make meals out of lizards, birds, and small mammals.

ANSWER: **True**

MANY SPIDERS MAKE WEBS TO CATCH PREY AND DEFEND AGAINST PREDATORS. **After catching prey in their sticky web, some of these spiders roll up their webs and chow down.** The webs are made of protein-rich silk, which the spider's body breaks down to replenish its silk supply and make a new web. **Spiders can produce up to seven kinds of silk, each with a specific function.** One type is used to wrap its prey, another type protects its eggs, and the remaining five make the spider's web. **Though thin and stretchy, spiderwebs are quite strong. Some even last years!**

Instant Genius

There are more than 45,000 species of spiders on Earth.

Tarantula spider

True or False:

Bones

are the only human body parts that don't contain water.

#15

Has anyone seen my water bottle?

37

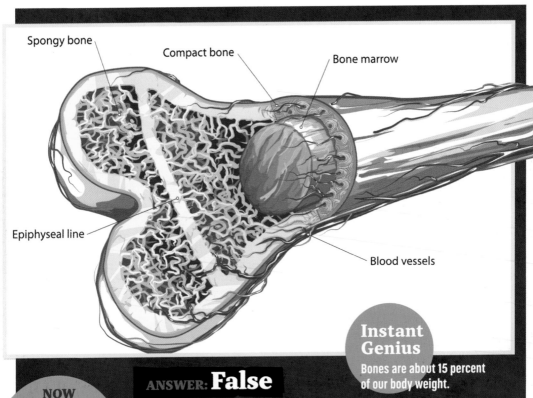

Spongy bone

Compact bone

Bone marrow

Epiphyseal line

Blood vessels

ANSWER: False

NOW YOU KNOW!
There are two types of bone tissue: the compact, hard outer shell and the spongy, flexible tissue inside.

OUR BONES CONTAIN 31 PERCENT WATER. BONES SUPPORT AND GIVE SHAPE TO OUR BODIES. They also help our bodies move and protect our organs. **Bones need water to function properly. Many cells also start in our bones, and they need water to form.** In the center of the bones is a spongy substance called marrow, which manufactures stem cells that in turn produce red blood cells that carry oxygen, white blood cells that fight infections, and platelets that help blood clot. **Bones store calcium, phosphorus, and other minerals that help your body grow and stay healthy.** They also store some fat that our bodies may need for later.

What is the most remote place on Earth?

a. Eagle Point

b. Point Reyes

c. Point Nemo

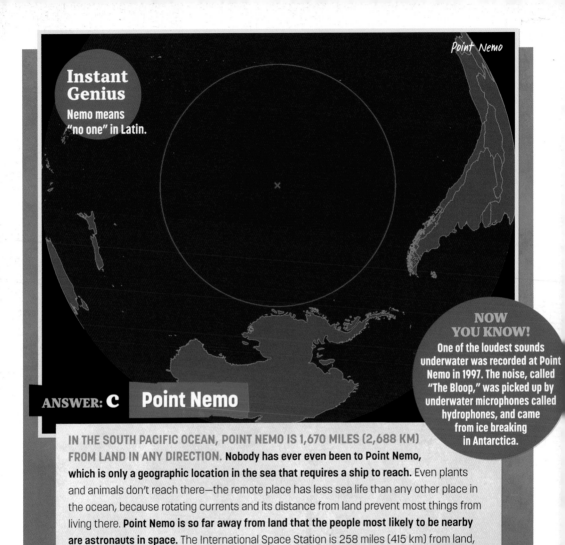

Point Nemo

NOW YOU KNOW!

One of the loudest sounds underwater was recorded at Point Nemo in 1997. The noise, called "The Bloop," was picked up by underwater microphones called hydrophones, and came from ice breaking in Antarctica.

ANSWER: C **Point Nemo**

IN THE SOUTH PACIFIC OCEAN, POINT NEMO IS 1,670 MILES (2,688 KM) FROM LAND IN ANY DIRECTION. Nobody has ever even been to Point Nemo, which is only a geographic location in the sea that requires a ship to reach. Even plants and animals don't reach there—the remote place has less sea life than any other place in the ocean, because rotating currents and its distance from land prevent most things from living there. **Point Nemo is so far away from land that the people most likely to be nearby are astronauts in space.** The International Space Station is 258 miles (415 km) from land, but Point Nemo is more than six times as far. **Sometimes called the "spacecraft graveyard," the site is often used as a crash-landing place for old spacecraft.**

#17

How many days does the **Tour de France** last?

a. 1   b. 23   c. 10

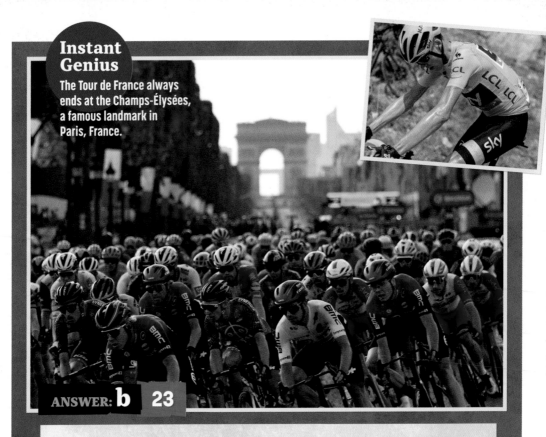

ANSWER: b   **23**

THE TOUR DE FRANCE IS A CYCLING RACE THAT COVERS MORE THAN 2,000 MILES (3,219 KM) AND LASTS 23 DAYS. There are 21 race days, called "stages"—each lasting up to six hours—and two rest days. The rider who is leading the competition at the beginning of a stage gets to wear a yellow jersey, which helps viewers keep an eye on the cyclist. A white jersey is awarded to the fastest rider under age 26, a polka-dotted jersey goes to the fastest person on the mountain section, and a green jersey is given for the most points earned for sprints and mini races in each stage. **At the end of the 23 days, the winner of the Tour de France is determined by adding up all the race times. Whoever has the shortest total time wins.**

How many grooves are on a U.S. quarter?

a. 19

b. 100

c. 119

NOW YOU KNOW!

There are 118 reeds on a dime. Grooves help distinguish coins that may otherwise look similar, such as nickels, which don't have ridges.

ANSWER: C 119

THERE ARE 119 GROOVES, CALLED REEDS, AROUND THE EDGE OF A U.S. QUARTER. **The reeds were added in the 1790s, when gold and silver coins were used as currency.** Before reeds were added, some people would secretly shave the sides of the coins to collect the filings of the valuable metals, hoping the next person to receive the coin wouldn't notice. **The metal shavings could be sold or used to make more coins.** The reeds prevented people from altering the edges, because it would be more noticeable. **Today, U.S. coins are made from zinc, copper, and nickel—but quarters and dimes still have reeds.**

Instant Genius

Great Britain and other European countries had ridges on their coins before the United States did.

44

All puppies
are born deaf.

#19

Say what?

ANSWER: **True**

ALL PUPPIES ARE BORN DEAF, AND THEIR HEARING IS THE LAST SENSE TO FULLY DEVELOP. **Puppies can finally hear at about three weeks old—and once they do, they can hear four times better than humans.** Dogs can also hear more frequencies, both higher and lower, than humans can. **But at birth, a puppy's ear canals are closed and their ability to hear is still developing.** Puppies are also born without fully formed sight and brain function. **For these to completely develop before birth, mother dogs would have a much longer pregnancy. In the wild, pregnancy slows down dogs and makes it harder to hunt.** Dogs continue to develop after birth so that their mom can go back to hunting sooner.

Instant Genius
Puppies don't open their eyes until they are about two to three weeks old.

46

#20

How many
ribs
do most
humans
have?

a. 8

b. 12

c. 24

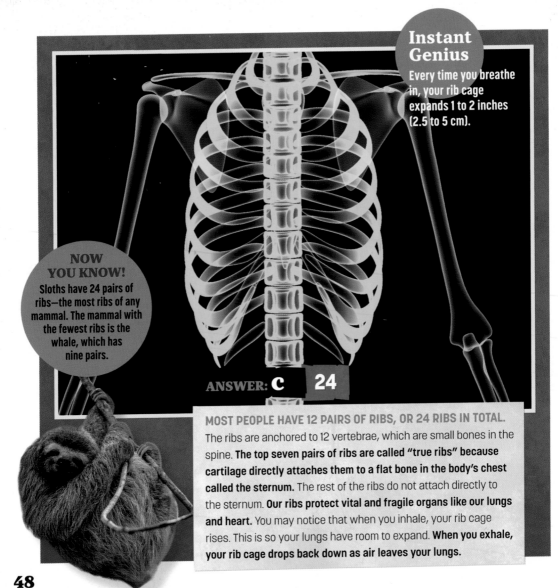

ANSWER: C 24

MOST PEOPLE HAVE 12 PAIRS OF RIBS, OR 24 RIBS IN TOTAL. The ribs are anchored to 12 vertebrae, which are small bones in the spine. **The top seven pairs of ribs are called "true ribs" because cartilage directly attaches them to a flat bone in the body's chest called the sternum.** The rest of the ribs do not attach directly to the sternum. **Our ribs protect vital and fragile organs like our lungs and heart.** You may notice that when you inhale, your rib cage rises. This is so your lungs have room to expand. **When you exhale, your rib cage drops back down as air leaves your lungs.**

Liquids

can't form
puddles in space.

NASA astronaut Jessica Meir watches water float by in the International Space Station.

ANSWER: True

THE LAWS OF PHYSICS IN SPACE ARE VERY DIFFERENT THAN THEY ARE ON EARTH. On Earth, gravity pulls everything to the planet's core. **As liquid is pulled downward, it takes the shape of its container.** In outer space, there is so little gravity that liquid and other things aren't tugged downward. Instead, the surface tension of the water molecules draws them as close together as possible, forming a bubble-like sphere rather than a puddle. **In space, air is no lighter than water, so if air is inside the sphere, it will look like a bubble within a bubble!**

NOW YOU KNOW!
There is gravity in space. Because it's a tiny amount —only one-thousandth of the gravity we have on Earth—it's called microgravity.

What is cryotherapy?

a. the use of extreme cold to treat injuries

b. the use of extreme heat to treat injuries

c. the feeling you get after a good cry

51

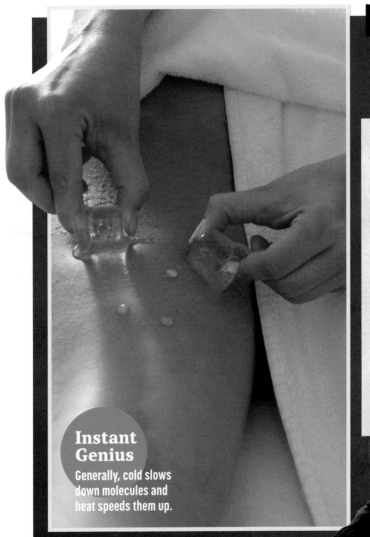

the use of extreme cold to treat injuries

CRYOTHERAPY IS THE USE OF EXTREME COLD TO TREAT SORENESS AND SWELLING FROM INJURIES. The practice dates back to 3000 BC, when ancient Egyptians put snow and ice on their wounds. The cold reduces bleeding by cooling the body's tissues that collect blood and slowing down swelling. Much later, in the 1800s, a British surgeon mixed salt and ice and used the concoction to shrink tumors and reduce pain. With the discovery of liquid nitrogen, cryotherapy got even colder. **Freezing cells this way causes them to die, so doctors often use the treatment to remove skin conditions such as dark spots or warts.**

Instant Genius

Generally, cold slows down molecules and heat speeds them up.

Why do **cats** stop eating before their bowls are empty?

#23

a. boredom **b.** stressed whiskers **c.** full stomachs

53

ANSWER: b **stressed whiskers**

CATS CAN TEMPORARILY WEAR OUT THEIR WHISKERS—A CONDITION KNOWN AS WHISKER FATIGUE. **Cat whiskers have special sensors that feel and relay information about the cats' surroundings to their brain.** For example, cats rely on their whiskers to navigate safely around furniture in the dark. **Cats get whisker fatigue when their sensitive whiskers are overstimulated, such as when cats constantly touch the sides of a bowl while eating.** As a result the cat might stop eating, and might instead pace around or paw at the bowl. Some cats try to eat only the food in the center of the bowl, so their whiskers don't touch the sides. **Really clever kitties might also use their paws to tip the bowl toward them, avoiding the sides altogether.**

Pinecones
can predict the weather.

ANSWER: **True**

PINECONES ARE HYGROMETERS, WHICH MEANS THEY CAN MEASURE THE AMOUNT OF WATER IN THE AIR. This is true for pinecones still growing on the tree, as well as those that have fallen to the ground. When it is cold and wet outside, the scales of a pinecone will be tightly closed, but in warm, dry weather the scales open. **Why? The pinecones' scales protect small, lightweight seeds.** On dry days, the scales open, allowing the seeds to fly away with the wind to grow in other parts of a forest. If the scales opened on a cold, wet day, the seeds would absorb moisture and land under the tree. **This is less than ideal, because the little seeds would have to compete with their parent tree for resources like water and nutrients in the soil.**

Instant Genius

Pine nuts come from pinecones.

56

25

A dolphin's skin is thicker than an elephant's.

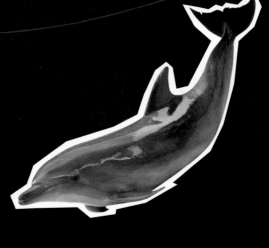

NOW YOU KNOW!

Dolphins eat up to 30 pounds (14 kg) of food each day. Sawfish, mackerel, squid, and herring are all part of the dolphin diet.

Instant Genius

Dolphin skin feels like rubber.

ANSWER: True

ELEPHANTS HAVE SKIN THAT'S ABOUT ONE INCH (2.5 CM) THICK, AND DOLPHIN SKIN IS TWO TO THREE TIMES THICKER! Dolphins shed the outer layer of their skin often, sometimes as frequently as every two hours—nine times more often than humans do. This helps keep their body smooth so dolphins can glide through the water with ease. **Dolphin skin is colored in a way to help them camouflage with their surroundings, even in the open ocean, through a method called countershading.** From above, their dark gray color is hard to see in the water. Their belly and underjaw are lighter in color, which helps them blend in with the sunlit ocean when viewed from beneath. **This conceals dolphins from predators as well as helps them sneak up on prey.**

Why is Africa known as the Cradle of Humankind?

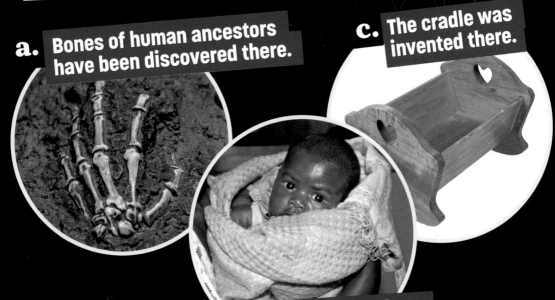

a. Bones of human ancestors have been discovered there.

b. More babies are born there than anywhere else.

c. The cradle was invented there.

NOW YOU KNOW!
When scientists find more complete fossils, they get to name them. A hominin fossil called Lucy, discovered in 1974, got its name from a late 1960s song.

ANSWER: a **Bones of human ancestors have been discovered there.**

Models of the skull of an early human

Instant Genius
More than a third of all early hominin fossils have been discovered at Sterkfontein.

THE EARLIEST EVIDENCE OF HUMAN LIFE, DATING BACK MORE THAN 3 MILLION YEARS, WAS DISCOVERED IN AFRICA. The Cradle of Humankind is a 180-square-mile (466 sq km) area in South Africa where archaeologists have unearthed prehistoric tools, the first evidence of human-made fire, and even fossils of humans' earliest ancestors, called hominins. The region has 13 major fossil sites, including the most famous, called Sterkfontein. In the 1930s, when the area was being mined for natural resources, hominin fossils were first unearthed. **Two of the most significant finds were discovered in the caves at Sterkfontein: a skull known as Mrs. Ples and a skeleton known as Little Foot, both dating back millions of years, which gave scientists clues about human evolution.**

Which country has the most pet dogs?

c. United States

a. China

b. Russia

ANSWER: C **United States**

NOW YOU KNOW!
In 2020, the American Kennel Club found that the Labrador retriever was the most popular dog breed. They've held the number one spot since 1991.

THERE ARE MORE THAN 75 MILLION PET PUPS IN THE UNITED STATES, WITH 44 PERCENT OF FAMILIES OWNING ONE, ACCORDING TO A 2017 SURVEY. Why so many pet pups? Having a dog has many benefits. **Petting a dog can lower heart rate and blood pressure.** Dogs need frequent walking, which also gets owners out exercising. Pets can even provide comfort to people with depression and anxiety. **More and more, owners view their pets as part of the family.** In fact, one survey found that one-third of Americans thought that animals should have as many rights to control their bodies as people do.

Llamas

are helping scientists research ways to treat COVID-19.

#28

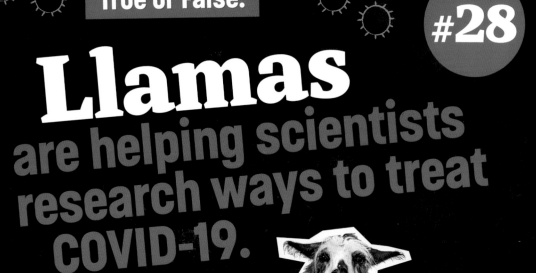

Instant Genius

Llamas are sometimes trained as therapy animals to help comfort sick people.

ANSWER: True

TO FIGHT OFF DISEASE, HUMANS AND OTHER MAMMALS RELY ON ANTIBODIES—PROTEINS OUR IMMUNE SYSTEM PRODUCES WHEN IT DETECTS A THREAT. **Llamas, like alpacas and camels, produce a special type of antibody called nanobodies.** Nanobodies are much smaller than antibodies, making them important to scientists researching treatments for COVID-19. In the past, scientists have used llama nanobodies to help with other respiratory illnesses, including severe acute respiratory syndrome, commonly known as SARS. **The viral protein that causes COVID-19, SARS-CoV-2, is covered in spikes, which enables it to fuse with a healthy cell. Once it's entered that cell, the virus replicates, producing more and more copies of itself.** Scientists are creating llama nanobodies that can bind tightly to the coronavirus protein and prevent it from invading a host cell, which could be given to humans to stop the virus from being harmful.

64

29

The Cuvier's beaked whale can hold its breath for how many hours?

a. about 1 hour

b. more than 3 hours

c. more than 6 hours

Instant Genius

Beaked whales have up to 14 different compartments in their stomach.

NOW YOU KNOW!

The world record holder for the longest time a person has voluntarily held their breath is 24 minutes and 37.36 seconds.

ANSWER: b more than 3 hours

A CUVIER'S BEAKED WHALE WAS ONCE RECORDED HOLDING ITS BREATH FOR AN INCREDIBLE 3 HOURS AND 42 MINUTES—LONGER THAN MOST MOVIES! On average, these whales hold their breath for about an hour at a time. **This ability enables them to swim to nearly 10,000 feet (3,000 m) below the ocean's surface without running out of air.** At these lower depths that other animals can't reach, the whales can find their favorite food—squid. **Scientists think the whales may stop the blood flow to certain organs to do this, so they can send oxygenated blood to their hearts, muscles, and brains instead.** They may also be able to lower their heart rates and might have a special type of muscle tissue that doesn't need as much oxygen as that of other mammals.

Which site is one of the New Seven Wonders of the World?

#30

c. Machu Picchu in Peru

a. Statue of Liberty in New York, U.S.A.

b. Acropolis in Athens, Greece

Machu Picchu, Peru

ANSWER: C **Machu Picchu in Peru**

THE NEW SEVEN WONDERS OF THE WORLD IS A POPULARITY POLL OF THE MOST IMPORTANT MONUMENTS AROUND THE GLOBE. The latest list includes the Great Wall of China, the Mayan city of Chichén Itzá, the ancient city of Petra in Jordan, the statue of Christ the Redeemer in Rio, the Roman Colosseum, the Taj Mahal in India, and Machu Picchu in Peru. Sitting more than 7,000 feet (2,130 km) above sea level in the Andes Mountains, the 15th-century site of Machu Picchu has 150 buildings, including temples, sanctuaries, houses, baths, and an observatory. Many archaeologists believe the site acted as the center for a royal Incan estate for emperors and nobles. Today, Machu Picchu remains one of the best-preserved ancient Incan cities in the world.

What gives saltwater crocodiles their deadly bite?

a. the size of their mouth

b. the strength of their jaws

c. the length of their teeth

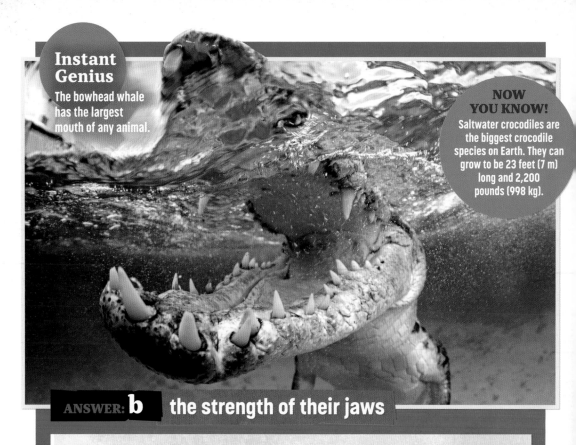

NOW YOU KNOW!

Saltwater crocodiles are the biggest crocodile species on Earth. They can grow to be 23 feet (7 m) long and 2,200 pounds (998 kg).

ANSWER: b the strength of their jaws

SALTWATER CROCODILES HAVE A BITE FORCE OF 16,460 NEWTONS, A UNIT OF MEASUREMENT NAMED AFTER ENGLISH PHYSICIST AND MATHEMATICIAN SIR ISAAC NEWTON. **To put it in perspective, our molars bite at a maximum force of 1,317 newtons—so crocs bite 12.5 times harder!** To figure this out, scientists had different crocodiles bite a contraption that looked like a metal sandwich, which could register the force of the bite. **Saltwater crocodiles won the competition, not for their tooth or mouth size, but for their large, specialized jaw muscles with fibers arranged to maximize the strength of their bite.** Far from picky eaters, saltwater crocodiles—native to India, Australia, and Southeast Asia—eat monkeys, water buffalo, boars, sharks, and even humans.

#32

True or False:

Mars
makes a humming noise.

MARS IS MAKING HUMMING NOISES—AND SCIENTISTS DON'T KNOW WHY. The sounds were detected through a robot on Mars called InSight. This robot was able to pick up a sound that would be impossible for humans to hear because it's humming at a higher frequency than we can detect. **Earth also hums because of ocean sounds and waves crashing onshore.** However, Mars's hum is unusually high-pitched. On Mars, the humming has nothing to do with oceans or winds, because they don't exist there. **However, the noise could have something to do with periodic earthquakes that happen on Mars, called "marsquakes."**

NOW YOU KNOW!

The Mars InSight lander also discovered a very strong magnetic field around Mars that protects the planet from potentially harmful radiation.

Instant Genius

On Mars, you could jump three times higher than on Earth. That's because the gravity on Mars is one-third the gravity on Earth.

Which country has built the most cars?

c. China

SAIC MOT

SAIC

a. United States

GM General Motors

TOYOTA

b. Japan

General Motors assembly line

ANSWER: C China

CHINA WILL HAVE BUILT 35 MILLION VEHICLES BY 2025—THE MOST OF ANY COUNTRY IN HISTORY. Cars were first made in the 1800s in Europe. By the early 1900s, with the help of assembly lines, the United States became the car industry leader. Since 2009, China has taken the lead, exceeding the amount of cars produced by the United States and Japan combined. **China is responsible for making more than 30 percent of cars around the world, including many electric vehicles.** Assembly lines are still used today to manufacture cars. But now robots, not humans, put the pieces together.

Ford assembly line, Michigan, 1928

NOW YOU KNOW!
By 2025, Chinese manufacturers also hope to be making nearly as many electric cars as are made in all of North America.

How many
muscles does
it take to
smile?

a. **2**

b. **6**

c. **12**

Scientists have found that smiles are more contagious than frowns. That's because smiling activates feel-good chemicals in the brain that decrease stress, relax the body, and elevate mood.

ANSWER: c 12

IT TAKES 12 MUSCLES TO SMILE. Four of these muscles pull the corners of the mouth up. Two muscles cause the skin around the eyes to crinkle, and two more muscles pull up your lips and nose. Then two other muscles angle your mouth up, and the last two pull your mouth out to the side. Although that's certainly a mouthful of muscles, they all work together to help you beam a happy smile. Despite what you might've heard, frowning takes one or two fewer muscles. **But scientists say it's easier to smile, because people do it more often, so our smiling muscles get more practice.** A real smile makes our eyes squint, and 99 percent of people cannot control this special eye movement that happens when we truly smile.

Facial muscles

#35

Spittlebugs
live in a home
that's made with their own pee.

A spittlebug (or froghopper)

Instant Genius

Spittlebugs are pests on farms because they take water from crops.

ANSWER: **True**

NOW YOU KNOW!

Adult spittlebugs are also known as froghoppers because they look like frogs. They can also jump more than 2 feet (0.6 m) high!

SPITTLEBUGS ARE TINY INSECTS THAT FEED ON PLANT SAP. Because plant sap is mostly water, spittlebugs must suck up enormous amounts of it to get the nutrients they need. That also means they produce a lot of urine. **As they pee, spittlebugs mix their urine with a sticky substance from their glands while also blowing air into the mixture from their abdomens to create a protective foam.** Spittlebugs are exothermic, which means their body temperature matches the temperature of their surroundings. **So, when temperatures in the spittlebugs' environment change, so do their body temperatures. Scientists found that spittlebug "cocoons" take on the same temperature as the surrounding cool soil.** The cocoons help the bugs stay cool and hydrated, as well as hidden from predators.

What is the world's longest mountain range?

c. The Andes

a. The Rockies

b. The Himalaya

Andes Mountains, Chile

Instant Genius

Most of the peaks of the Andes Mountains are volcanic.

ANSWER: C **The Andes**

THE ANDES ARE THE LONGEST CONTINENTAL MOUNTAIN RANGE IN THE WORLD, STRETCHING 4,700 MILES (7,564 KM) FROM NORTH TO SOUTH. The mountain range crosses seven South American countries and is divided into three sections: the southern Andes in Chile and Argentina; the central Andes in Peru and Bolivia; and the northern Andes that run through Ecuador, Columbia, and Venezuela. **The Andes also have some of the world's highest mountains outside of Asia, with an average height of 13,000 feet (3,962 m).**

37

How do small tugboats pull huge ships?

a. They use the huge ship's motor.

b. They have a very powerful motor.

c. They use the water's current.

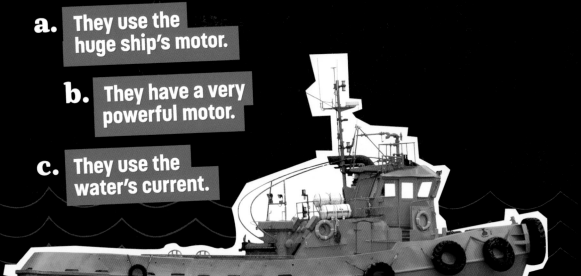

British inventor Jonathan Hulls invented the tugboat in 1736.

ANSWER: b

They have a very powerful motor.

NOW YOU KNOW!

The golden age for pirates was between 1650 and 1720. During this time, bands of pirates raided ships looking for treasure in the Caribbean Sea and Indian Ocean.

SMALL TUGBOATS CAN PULL OR PUSH MUCH LARGER SHIPS BECAUSE THEY HAVE VERY POWERFUL MOTORS. **A tugboat's engines and propellers give them great force to let them change directions and steer big ships.** There are two categories of tugboats: inland tugboats and oceanic tugboats. **Inland tugboats go into shallow waters like rivers and harbors, to assist large ships as they come into port. Oceanic tugboats help large ships maneuver in the open sea.** Some tugboats are also equipped with icebreaking technology. They can crash through ice to let big boats pass through behind them. **Tugboats also help move boats that have no motors or propellers, which are called "dumb boats."** Dumb boats do not have any speed but can transport a lot of weight, such as materials, goods, floating docks, and even people—thanks to tugboats moving them.

Which **rodent** lives the longest?

a. chinchilla

b. naked mole rat

c. hamster

Who are you calling Gramps?

ANSWER: **b**

naked mole rat

THE NAKED MOLE RAT IS AS TINY AS A MOUSE AND CAN LIVE FOR UP TO 30 YEARS—LONGER THAN ANY OTHER RODENT. Naked mole rats also don't seem to get age-related illnesses and have powerful cancer-defending cells compared to other animals. Scientists are studying them to determine how they live such long and healthy lives. **Naked mole rats live in eastern Africa in groups called colonies. Each colony has just one breeding female, called the queen.** Mole rats burrow very far underground, so they don't have to worry about many predators. **A colony's tunnel can stretch 2.5 miles (4 km) long.** If a predator like a snake does come along, the colonies have mole rats designated as guards to defend them.

Instant Genius

Naked mole rats hydrate by eating plant roots and tubers, which contain water.

Human activity
can affect clouds.

#39

NOW YOU KNOW!
The Cloud Appreciation Society is a worldwide organization of people who share information about the clouds they see.

Clouds from dust storms, like this one in Arizona, happen naturally. Clouds that form due to human activity are called anthropogenic clouds.

ANSWER: True

Instant Genius
Some clouds can weigh 1.1 million pounds (499,000 kg).

CLOUDS FORM WHEN WATER THAT HAS EVAPORATED FROM EARTH COOLS AND CONDENSES AROUND MICROSCOPIC PARTICLES CALLED AEROSOLS. Most aerosols occur naturally, like desert dust, salt from the oceans, and smoke from forest fires. Humans create the rest, such as by car exhaust and emissions from power plants. Some aerosols reflect sunlight, which allows the clouds to block heat from the sun and keep Earth's atmosphere cooler. Other aerosols, especially human-made ones, absorb and trap heat on Earth, which warms the atmosphere. Scientists who study climate can learn about global warming by studying clouds.

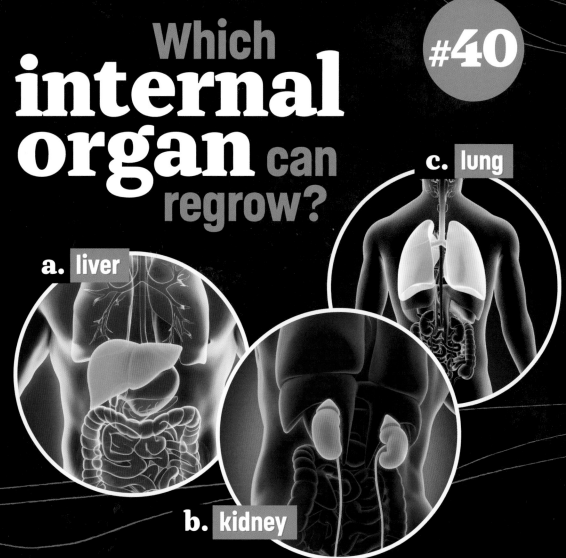

Which internal organ can regrow?

c. lung

a. liver

b. kidney

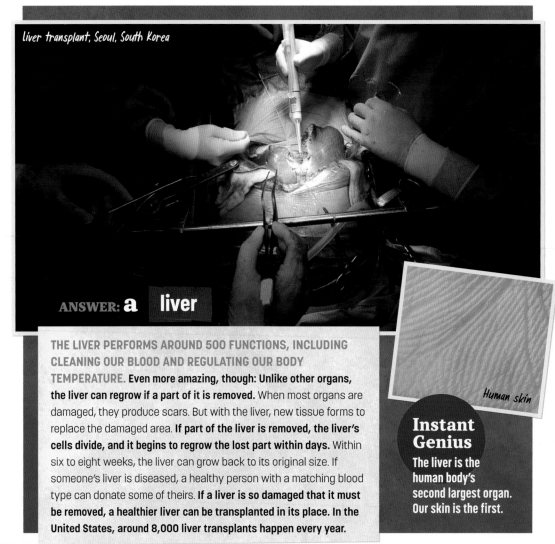

liver transplant, Seoul, South Korea

ANSWER: a liver

Human skin

THE LIVER PERFORMS AROUND 500 FUNCTIONS, INCLUDING CLEANING OUR BLOOD AND REGULATING OUR BODY TEMPERATURE. **Even more amazing, though: Unlike other organs, the liver can regrow if a part of it is removed.** When most organs are damaged, they produce scars. But with the liver, new tissue forms to replace the damaged area. **If part of the liver is removed, the liver's cells divide, and it begins to regrow the lost part within days.** Within six to eight weeks, the liver can grow back to its original size. If someone's liver is diseased, a healthy person with a matching blood type can donate some of theirs. **If a liver is so damaged that it must be removed, a healthier liver can be transplanted in its place. In the United States, around 8,000 liver transplants happen every year.**

Instant Genius

The liver is the human body's second largest organ. Our skin is the first.

Sharks

don't have bones.

How 'bout lunch?

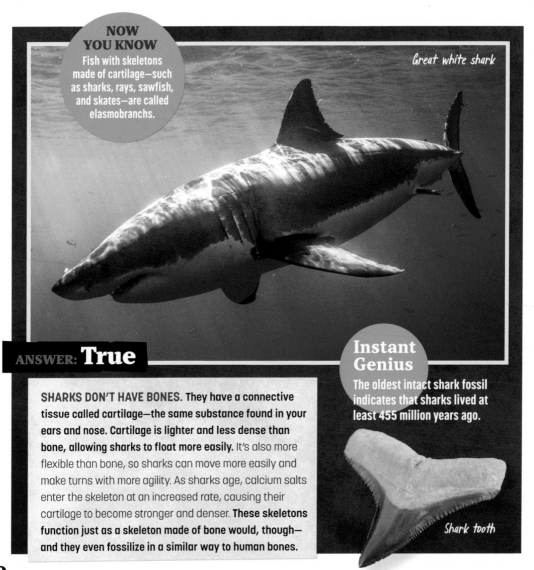

Great white shark

ANSWER: **True**

SHARKS DON'T HAVE BONES. They have a connective tissue called cartilage—the same substance found in your ears and nose. Cartilage is lighter and less dense than bone, allowing sharks to float more easily. It's also more flexible than bone, so sharks can move more easily and make turns with more agility. As sharks age, calcium salts enter the skeleton at an increased rate, causing their cartilage to become stronger and denser. **These skeletons function just as a skeleton made of bone would, though—and they even fossilize in a similar way to human bones.**

Instant Genius

The oldest intact shark fossil indicates that sharks lived at least 455 million years ago.

Shark tooth

What is the closest major galaxy to the **Milky Way?**

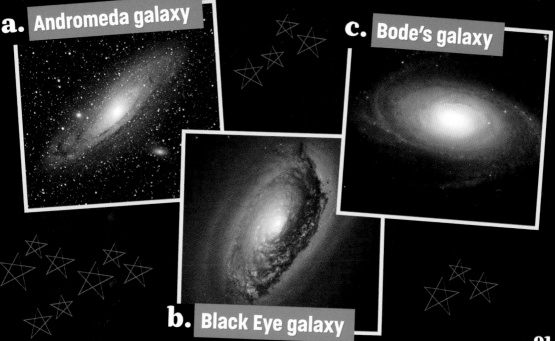

a. Andromeda galaxy

c. Bode's galaxy

b. Black Eye galaxy

Andromeda galaxy

ANSWER: a **Andromeda galaxy**

CASSIOPEIA

SEGIN (ε)

RUCHBAH (δ)   NAVI (γ)   CAPH (β)

ACHIRD (η)

SCHEDAR (α)

PACMAN NEBULA

ALTHOUGH NEARBY ARE A COUPLE OF DWARF GALAXIES, WHICH ARE DIMMER AND SMALLER IN SIZE, THE CLOSEST MAJOR GALAXY TO THE MILKY WAY IS ANDROMEDA. This galaxy is so bright, it's the farthest object in the night sky that's visible without special telescopes. Though you can't see it moving from 2.5 million light-years away, the Milky Way and Andromeda galaxies are on a collision course. They are heading toward each other at about 70 miles (113 km) a second. When they finally fly past each other, their dark matter will tangle and get snagged, and they may fuse together into one mega-galaxy. Scientists are using a telescope to measure Andromeda's motion and predict when the collision will happen. But don't worry, this won't happen for another 4 billion years!

Instant Genius

Stargazers can find Andromeda by looking for constellations near it, such as the Great Square of Pegasus or Cassiopeia.

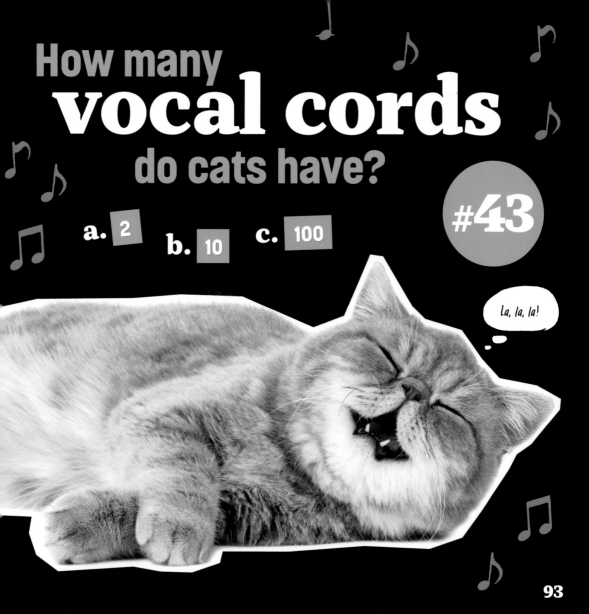

How many **vocal cords** do cats have?

a. 2   b. 10   c. 100

#43

la, la, la!

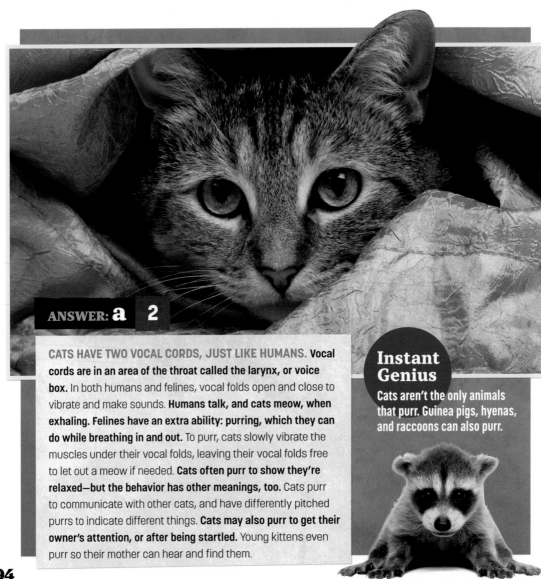

CATS HAVE TWO VOCAL CORDS, JUST LIKE HUMANS. Vocal cords are in an area of the throat called the larynx, or voice box. In both humans and felines, vocal folds open and close to vibrate and make sounds. **Humans talk, and cats meow, when exhaling. Felines have an extra ability: purring, which they can do while breathing in and out.** To purr, cats slowly vibrate the muscles under their vocal folds, leaving their vocal folds free to let out a meow if needed. **Cats often purr to show they're relaxed—but the behavior has other meanings, too.** Cats purr to communicate with other cats, and have differently pitched purrs to indicate different things. **Cats may also purr to get their owner's attention, or after being startled.** Young kittens even purr so their mother can hear and find them.

Instant Genius

Cats aren't the only animals that purr. Guinea pigs, hyenas, and raccoons can also purr.

Beavers

were once the size of bears.

Instant Genius

Giant beavers were North America's largest living rodents during their time.

ANSWER: **True**

NOW YOU KNOW!

Megalonyx sloths, which roamed Earth at the same time as giant beavers, were up to 9.8 feet (3 m) long.

ABOUT 1.4 MILLION YEARS AGO, BEAVERS WERE THE SIZE OF BLACK BEARS. Scientists discovered the giant beaver fossils in Florida, Alaska, Indiana, and Illinois, U.S.A. The giant beavers had long, thin tails instead of the paddle-shaped ones they have today. **They also had rounded front teeth with blunt tips, unlike the sharp, chisel-like teeth of modern beavers.** Giant beavers died off 10,000 years ago, around the same time as other large mammals like the woolly mammoth. Scientists think this is because the giant beavers relied on wetland habitat for both food and shelter. **At the end of the last ice age, Earth became much hotter and drier, and the giant beavers could no longer survive.**

How fast can the world's current **fastest human run?**

a. 20 miles (32 km) an hour

b. 27 miles (43 km) an hour

c. 37 miles (60 km) an hour

Usain Bolt (center) takes the lead during a race in London, England.

ANSWER: b

27 miles (43 km) an hour

USAIN BOLT HOLDS THE RECORD FOR BEING THE FASTEST HUMAN. He can run 27.78 miles (45 km) an hour in a 100-meter sprint. Running uses 200 muscles, which are crucial to an athlete's speed. **When running, most people are on the ground for almost half the time, exerting force to push themselves into the air.** The other half of the time is spent in the air, and a runner is propelled forward during this time. **Compared to the average human, elite athletes' strong muscles help them push off the ground more quickly with each stride, and they spend closer to 60 percent of their running time in the air.**

Which part of a **pigeon** weighs the most?

#46

a. bones

b. feathers

c. beak

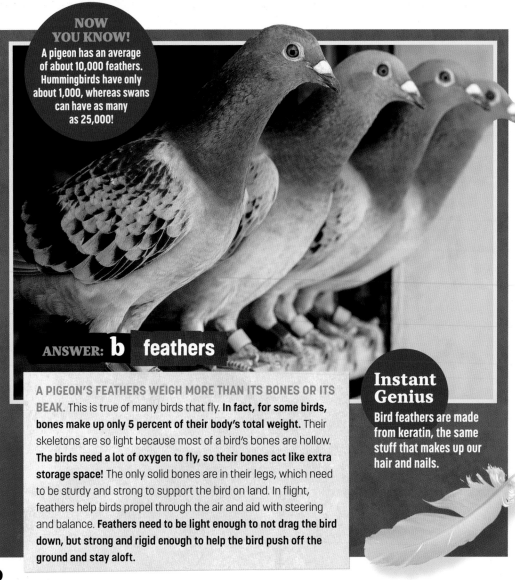

NOW YOU KNOW!

A pigeon has an average of about 10,000 feathers. Hummingbirds have only about 1,000, whereas swans can have as many as 25,000!

ANSWER: b feathers

A PIGEON'S FEATHERS WEIGH MORE THAN ITS BONES OR ITS BEAK. This is true of many birds that fly. **In fact, for some birds, bones make up only 5 percent of their body's total weight.** Their skeletons are so light because most of a bird's bones are hollow. **The birds need a lot of oxygen to fly, so their bones act like extra storage space!** The only solid bones are in their legs, which need to be sturdy and strong to support the bird on land. In flight, feathers help birds propel through the air and aid with steering and balance. **Feathers need to be light enough to not drag the bird down, but strong and rigid enough to help the bird push off the ground and stay aloft.**

Instant Genius

Bird feathers are made from keratin, the same stuff that makes up our hair and nails.

Doing
good deeds
can make you happy.

#47

Volunteers

ANSWER: True

ACCORDING TO SCIENTIFIC STUDIES, DOING SOMETHING NICE FOR OTHERS NOT ONLY BRINGS THEM HAPPINESS—IT CAN ALSO BOOST YOUR OWN MOOD. **This is because certain areas of the brain are activated to release chemicals called endorphins, which make us feel good.** Helping others can make us feel like we are part of a community, which also has health benefits. **Other factors that contribute to a sense of well-being include getting a good night's sleep, being outdoors, listening to music, and having a positive attitude. Now that's cheerful news!**

Instant Genius

People who spend time with happy people feel happier themselves, according to a study.

A metal can be a gas.

#48

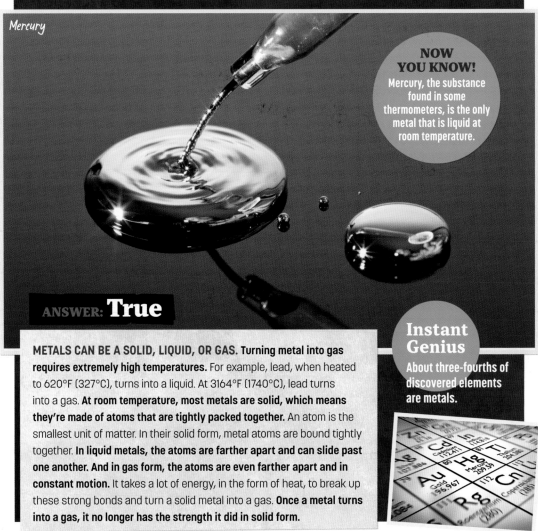

Mercury

ANSWER: **True**

Instant Genius
About three-fourths of discovered elements are metals.

METALS CAN BE A SOLID, LIQUID, OR GAS. Turning metal into gas requires extremely high temperatures. For example, lead, when heated to 620°F (327°C), turns into a liquid. At 3164°F (1740°C), lead turns into a gas. **At room temperature, most metals are solid, which means they're made of atoms that are tightly packed together.** An atom is the smallest unit of matter. In their solid form, metal atoms are bound tightly together. **In liquid metals, the atoms are farther apart and can slide past one another. And in gas form, the atoms are even farther apart and in constant motion.** It takes a lot of energy, in the form of heat, to break up these strong bonds and turn a solid metal into a gas. **Once a metal turns into a gas, it no longer has the strength it did in solid form.**

Periodic table of elements

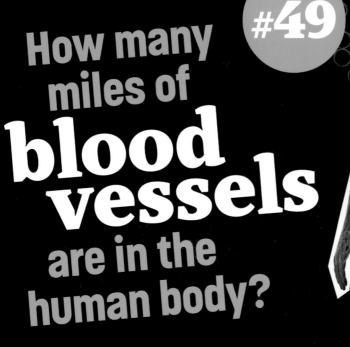

How many miles of **blood vessels** are in the human body?

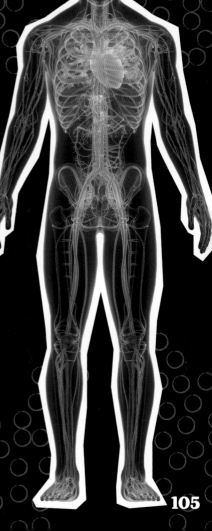

#49

a. 6 miles (9.6 km)

b. 60 miles (96 km)

c. 60,000 miles (96,561 km)

Red blood cells

ANSWER: C

60,000 miles (96,561 km)

THE HUMAN BODY HAS ABOUT 60,000 MILES (96,561 KM) OF BLOOD VESSELS, BROKEN DOWN INTO THREE TYPES: ARTERIES, CAPILLARIES, AND VEINS. Together, they help your heart pump blood into the body in a fast and orderly way. **Arteries take blood filled with nutrients and oxygen from the heart and distribute it through the body. The arteries transport that blood to tiny capillaries, which distribute oxygen and nutrients to the body's tissues while also absorbing carbon dioxide and other waste.** The capillaries connect to veins, which carry the deoxygenated blood back to the heart, disposing of waste products along the way. **Arteries and veins have a smooth exterior, which makes it easier for the blood to travel quickly.**

Hemoglobin molecule

Instant Genius

Blood gets its red color from a protein called hemoglobin.

What was
Meganeuropsis?

c. the smallest bird on Earth

a. the largest insect to ever fly

b. the fastest dinosaur on land

Meganeuropsis

NOW YOU KNOW!

Some scientists think oxygen levels in Earth's atmosphere were higher during the Paleozoic era, when *Meganeuropsis* lived. That could help explain how the insect grew to be so large.

ANSWER: **a** the largest insect to ever fly

MEGANEUROPSIS AMERICANA—THE ANCESTOR OF MODERN DRAGONFLIES—LIVED 275 MILLION YEARS AGO, BEFORE DINOSAURS EVER ROAMED AND BIRDS EVER FLEW. Though now extinct, it was the largest insect to ever fly! **In Oklahoma, U.S.A., in 1940, a scientist discovered the first fossil, which revealed that the ancient insect had a wingspan of 2.5 feet (0.7 m), roughly six times larger than most dragonflies today.** According to scientists, these giant insects mostly ate smaller insects and amphibians. It could operate each of its two pairs of wings independently, swooping down to snatch prey at speeds of up to 35 miles (56 km) an hour. **Like its modern-day relatives, *Meganeuropsis* had serrated, or sawlike, teeth to slice through its prey.**

True or False:

Oysters
can change their gender.

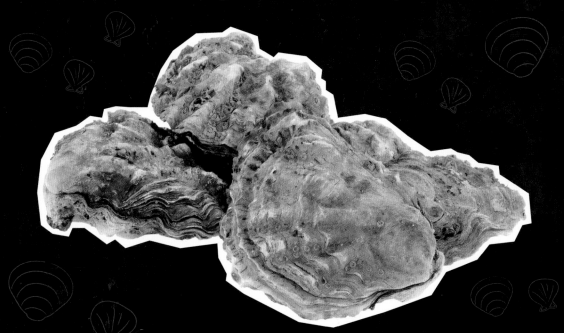

ANSWER: True

Instant Genius
Triggerfish can also change genders in the same way as oysters do.

OYSTERS ARE MOLLUSKS, WHICH HAVE SOFT BODIES INSIDE HARD, ROUGH SHELLS. They live in shallow seawater. Oysters can change from male to female or female to male many times throughout their lives. All oysters begin as male. By the age of one, most have permanently transitioned to female. However, they can switch again. Because oysters can be either gender, they don't need mates to reproduce. Instead, they fertilize their own eggs. The eggs that aren't fertilized become food for many other species in the ocean.

How many sides does a snowflake have?

a. 2

b. 6

c. 13

ANSWER: **b** 6

EVERY SNOWFLAKE HAS EXACTLY SIX SIDES. This is because the water molecules in its ice crystals always join one another in a hexagonal, or six-sided, arrangement. A snowflake starts as a single water droplet that has frozen into an ice crystal in the sky. **For a crystal to form, the temperature must be –31°F (–35°C) or lower. As the crystal falls through the air, it collects more water molecules that lump together to form a flake.** No two snowflakes are exactly alike, because variations in weather and temperature as they form are infinite. **But there are three basic shapes: dendrite, which has a detailed, branchlike structure; thin plate, which is flatter and less intricate; and sector, which has a star shape in the middle.**

NOW YOU KNOW!
The snowiest city in the world is Aomori City, Japan. It gets an average of 26 feet (8 m) of snowfall each year.

What does the word *astronaut* loosely mean in Greek?

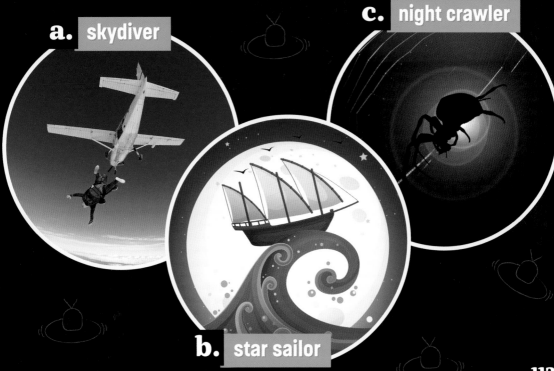

a. skydiver

c. night crawler

b. star sailor

Ahoy there, alien!

ANSWER: b **star sailor**

Instant Genius

The Russian word for astronaut—*cosmonaut*—comes from the Greek word *kosmos* for "universe."

50ₚ. POCCИЯ

RUSSIA·2011

THE WORD *ASTRONAUT* COMES FROM TWO GREEK WORDS THAT ROUGHLY TRANSLATE TO "STAR SAILOR." The first part, *astro,* comes from the Greek word *astron,* which means "star." The second part, *naut,* comes from the Greek word *nautes,* which means "sailor." On April 12, 1961, a Soviet man named Yuri Gagarin became the first astronaut in space. **Since then, more than 550 astronauts have sailed through the stars.**

#54

A stadium full of
fans can improve an
athlete's
performance.

GEICO

ANSWER: True

SPECTATORS ARE IMPORTANT TO PROFESSIONAL SPORTS BECAUSE, ACCORDING TO SCIENTISTS, PEOPLE ARE MORE LIKELY TO PERFORM BETTER IF OTHERS ARE WATCHING THEM. **Although crowds can be noisy, professional athletes are often trained to tune out the distractions.** One study found that sports teams are actually more likely to win if they have a bigger crowd cheering them on. **With audiences, players get additional adrenaline, which is energy produced by a hormone in the body.** Adrenaline is good for sports involving less precise movement, like speed skating and basketball. **However, it may also reduce concentration needed for sports that require more precise movements, like gymnastics and golf.**

Dogs stick their heads out of car windows to smell their surroundings.

#55

I smell pizza!

ANSWER: True

ALTHOUGH HUMANS MOSTLY RELY ON THE SENSE OF SIGHT, DOGS USE THEIR SENSE OF SMELL TO EXPERIENCE THE WORLD. When a dog sticks its head out of a car window, it's similar to a human looking out the window to take in new sights. **Once a dog has sniffed everything inside the car, it might stick its head out the window to detect new scents in the distance.** Dogs might also do this to feel the air on their faces, or to see where they are. As wind travels over a dog's nose, its scent receptors recognize smells. **Dogs can detect scents from up to 12 miles (20 km) away!**

How big was the largest hailstone ever recorded?

a. the size of a golf ball

b. the size of a softball

c. the size of a volleyball

Instant Genius

Storms with superstrong upward currents are called supercell thunderstorms.

ANSWER: c

the size of a volleyball

THE LARGEST HAILSTONE WAS RECORDED IN THE UNITED STATES AFTER IT LANDED IN SOUTH DAKOTA IN 2010. It was 8 inches (20 cm) wide and weighed nearly 2 pounds (0.9 kg)! In 2018, a storm in Argentina produced a hailstone that probably measured 7.4 to 9.3 inches (19 to 24 cm). A teenager kept and measured a piece, allowing scientists to see proof of the gigantic specimen. **Hailstones form during a storm when air currents carry water droplets upward into the atmosphere, where the water freezes.** A gargantuan hailstone requires a lot of upward-blowing wind to form. **Suspended in the air, the hailstone continues to grow into bigger and bigger chunks until the air can no longer support its weight and it falls to the ground.**

NOW YOU KNOW!

Colorado experiences more damage from hailstorms than any other state in the United States.

57

True or False:

Dolphins
don't live in Arctic or Antarctic waters.

ANSWER: **False**

ORCAS, A TYPE OF DOLPHIN, CAN SURVIVE IN THE COLD WATERS OF THE ARCTIC AND ANTARCTIC, THANKS TO THEIR LARGE SIZE AND A THICK LAYER OF BLUBBER. Orcas can reach 32 feet (10 m) long—almost as big as a school bus—and weigh up to 12,000 pounds (5,443 kg). Although similar in size to most whales, orcas are classified as dolphins because of their beak-shaped face and the dorsal fin on top of their body. **These cool creatures are found in oceans all over the world, but are most common in polar regions.** Other dolphins, such as the Arctic's white-beaked dolphins and the Antarctic's hourglass dolphins, sometimes swim in these frigid areas, too. **At the top of the food chain, orcas hunt in these polar waters for prey such as fish, seals, sea lions, penguins, and sometimes even whales!**

What was **Ada Lovelace** known for?

a. She started Valentine's Day.

c. She was the first computer programmer.

b. She invented shoelaces.

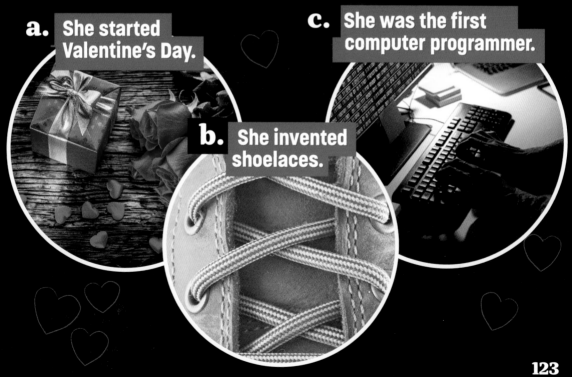

Ada Lovelace, English mathematician

Instant Genius

The computer programming language "Ada" is named after Ada Lovelace.

She was the first computer programmer.

ADA LOVELACE WAS FAMOUS FOR BEING THE WORLD'S FIRST COMPUTER PROGRAMMER. **Born in London in 1815, Ada Lovelace was the daughter of a famous poet, Lord Byron.** In the 1830s, mathematics professor Charles Babbage invented a machine that was used for mathematic calculations. **In 1843, Ada published an English translation of a French article about the computing machine, adding her own notes to the publication.** These notes included theories on how the machine could be used for more than mathematics. **She wrote about how computers could perform actions based on letters and symbols, in addition to numbers, to solve complex equations.** She also wrote about possible ways for a computer to loop codes and instructions in a repeating pattern. **This method, called looping, is used in computer programming today.**

ADA COUNTESS OF LOVELACE 1815–1852 Pioneer of Computing lived here

#59

Your skull's bones don't move.

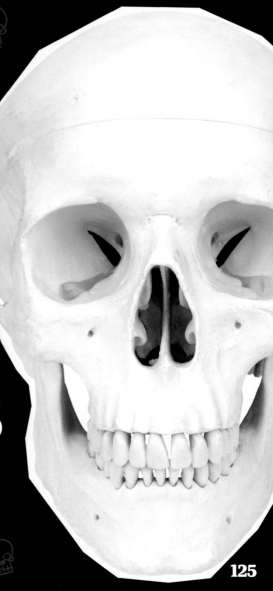

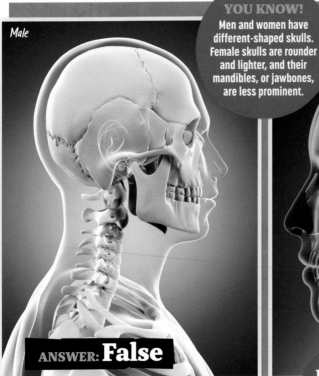

Male

Female

ANSWER: **False**

THE HUMAN SKULL, MADE OF 22 BONES, PROTECTS YOUR BRAIN AND FACE. **The part around the brain is called the cranium, and it has eight bones.** One of these, the frontal bone, forms your forehead. **Then, 14 skull bones protect your face. One of these, your mandible, is the only skull bone that moves.** Also called the jawbone, it's the bone that holds your lower teeth. The mandible goes up and down and side to side whenever you chew or talk. This is the strongest bone in your face.

Instant Genius

Some fish have 130 skull bones.

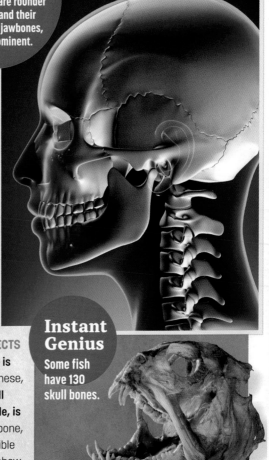

How did glass frogs get their name?

a. They shatter to escape predators.

b. Their skin is see-through.

c. They can produce glass.

I'm into hip-hop!

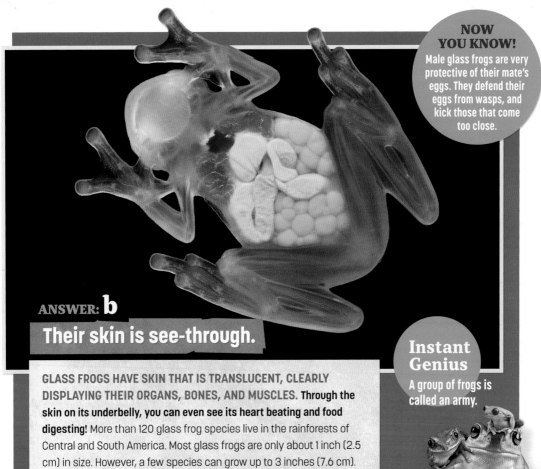

ANSWER: b

Their skin is see-through.

GLASS FROGS HAVE SKIN THAT IS TRANSLUCENT, CLEARLY DISPLAYING THEIR ORGANS, BONES, AND MUSCLES. **Through the skin on its underbelly, you can even see its heart beating and food digesting!** More than 120 glass frog species live in the rainforests of Central and South America. Most glass frogs are only about 1 inch (2.5 cm) in size. However, a few species can grow up to 3 inches (7.6 cm). Why these frogs have clear skin is still a mystery, but scientists think it could be to protect them from predators. **Their see-through skin helps them blend into their surroundings.** Some have green skin with spots, a pattern that makes them look like a clutch of tiny eggs. **When a hungry predator comes along, these sneaky amphibians can pretend to be a less-satisfying snack.**

Yodeling
can cause an
avalanche.

#61

Avalanches can zoom downhill at 100 miles (161 km) an hour. In 1970, a massive avalanche in Peru traveled up to 208 miles (335 km) an hour.

Shkhara Mountains, Russia

ANSWER: False

IT'S A MYTH THAT YODELING CAN CAUSE AN AVALANCHE, WHICH IS A MASS OF SNOW, ICE, AND ROCKS THAT FALL RAPIDLY DOWN A MOUNTAINSIDE. To bust the myth, some curious people did an experiment. **They brought a professional yodeler to Telluride, Colorado, to sing through a megaphone at a snowy peak. Nothing happened.** In the end, hundreds of pounds of explosives were used to dislodge nearby snowpack. **Weather conditions cause avalanches to happen naturally, but more than 90 percent of avalanches are due to human activity.** Climbers, skiers, and snowmobilers can all trigger massive slabs of snow to suddenly shatter and steamroll downhill. **But singers of all types don't play a role.**

Instant Genius
A small avalanche is called a slough.

130

Why do you often see rocks around train tracks?

a. to keep the tracks in place

b. to keep animals away

c. to absorb the weight of the trains

Vancouver to Calgary freight train, Canada

NOW YOU KNOW!

After U.S. president Abraham Lincoln's assassination in 1865, a funeral train carried his body back to his home state of Illinois, stopping in 180 cities along the way. This event popularized train travel.

Instant Genius

Trains were invented in Wales, part of the United Kingdom, in 1804.

9549

ANSWER: a to keep the tracks in place

TO KEEP THE TRACKS IN PLACE, THERE ARE ALMOST ALWAYS ROCKS, CALLED BALLAST, SURROUNDING TRAIN TRACKS. **The ballast keeps the wooden cross ties, which run perpendicular to the train's tracks, safely secured. Purposefully sharp, these rocks keep trains from rolling away from the tracks.** That's good, considering some trains and their cargo can weigh up to 1,000,000 pounds (454,000 kg)! Railroads are still considered the most efficient way to haul goods across Earth's surface, despite the many forms of modern vehicles. **That's especially true for bulky products, such as grain and coal, or heavy items, such as cars and trucks, because trains are a less expensive way to transport them.** The ballast also allows for more heat expansion and ground movement than a solid surface, and easily drains rain and snow and blocks weeds from growing.

THE NATION MOURNS.

BUFFALO AND ERIE RAIL ROAD

SPECIAL TIME TABLE

For Funeral Train conveying the Remains of the late President

ABRAHAM LINCOLN,

FROM BUFFALO TO ERIE,

THURSDAY, APRIL 20, 1865.

"The Nation Mourns," death notice for Abraham Lincoln, 1865

63

Racecar
drivers
are considered athletes.

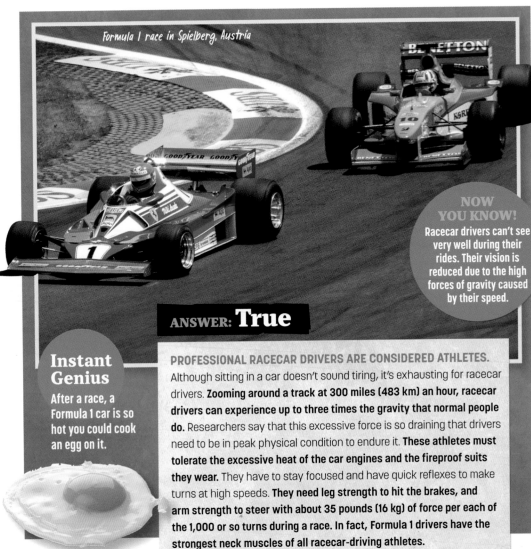

Formula 1 race in Spielberg, Austria

ANSWER: **True**

Instant Genius

After a race, a Formula 1 car is so hot you could cook an egg on it.

PROFESSIONAL RACECAR DRIVERS ARE CONSIDERED ATHLETES. Although sitting in a car doesn't sound tiring, it's exhausting for racecar drivers. **Zooming around a track at 300 miles (483 km) an hour, racecar drivers can experience up to three times the gravity that normal people do.** Researchers say that this excessive force is so draining that drivers need to be in peak physical condition to endure it. **These athletes must tolerate the excessive heat of the car engines and the fireproof suits they wear.** They have to stay focused and have quick reflexes to make turns at high speeds. **They need leg strength to hit the brakes, and arm strength to steer with about 35 pounds (16 kg) of force per each of the 1,000 or so turns during a race.** In fact, Formula 1 drivers have the strongest neck muscles of all racecar-driving athletes.

64

Who patented the
telephone?

a. Alexander Graham Bell

c. Nikola Tesla

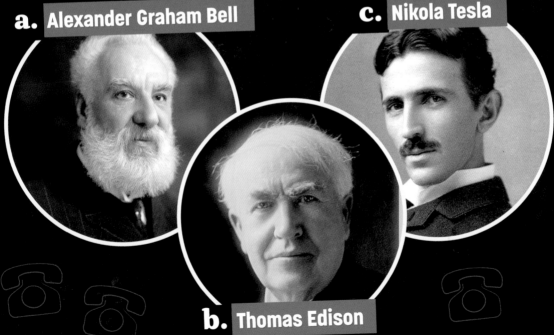

b. Thomas Edison

Alexander Graham Bell

Instant Genius

The word *telephone* comes from the Greek roots *tele*, meaning "far," and *phone*, meaning "sound."

Can you hear me now?

ANSWER: a **Alexander Graham Bell**

ALTHOUGH IT'S UNCLEAR WHO REALLY INVENTED THE FIRST TELEPHONE, BECAUSE SEVERAL PEOPLE WERE WORKING ON IT AT THE SAME TIME, THE CREDIT USUALLY GOES TO THE SCOTTISH-BORN INVENTOR ALEXANDER GRAHAM BELL. **He was the first to patent it, which means he established the rights to make and sell it.** In 1876, Bell figured out how to send electric currents through a wire. From that experiment, he discovered a way to transmit human speech through the wire. He got a patent for his invention, but Bell, and later other scientists, continued making improvements to the device. **Today, the basic technology of a telephone hasn't changed much, but the landlines that use it are becoming less common.** The wireless connections of our cell phones function more like radios than Bell's telephone.

136

How big are the eyes of a
giant squid?

a. the size of golf balls

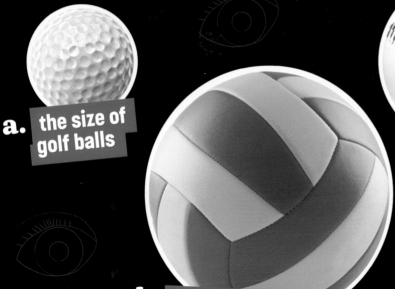

b. the size of volleyballs

c. the size of baseballs

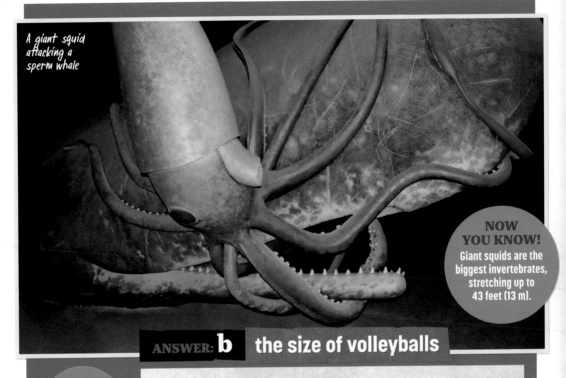

A giant squid attacking a sperm whale

ANSWER: b **the size of volleyballs**

Instant Genius
Squid eat crustaceans and fish, but sometimes they also eat each other.

THE EYES OF THE GIANT SQUID ARE EACH A WHOPPING 10 INCHES (25 CM) ACROSS—ABOUT THE SIZE OF VOLLEYBALLS! **These are the biggest eyes in the animal world. Giant squids use their enormous peepers to spot one of their predators, sperm whales.** One of the world's largest predators, sperm whales have excellent echolocation skills. By sending out signals that bounce back to them, sperm whales can quickly find prey from far away. **Luckily for the giant squid, its eyes can detect light, even in the depths of the ocean.** It's dark and hard for humans to see at such depths, but scientists think the giant squid might be able to see the shifting glow of crustaceans and jellyfish as they get knocked around by a sperm whale and scram to safety.

Why do dogs kick backward after they go to the bathroom?

a. to dig up a bone

#66

b. to hide their droppings

c. to spread around their scent

ANSWER: C

to spread around their scent

WHEN DOGS LEAVE DROPPINGS, THEY ARE MARKING THE AREA AS THEIR OWN. Dogs have glands on their feet that release pheromones, which are chemicals that create a specific smell. Many animals use pheromones to communicate. When dogs kick back their feet, they spread these pheromones from the glands in their paws to the ground, in addition to spreading the scent of their droppings. Along with the scent clues, flung dirt is a visual signal to other dogs that a dog has been there. Marking behavior is a warning for other dogs to stay off a pup's turf. It can also be a way of signaling to other dogs that the area is safe.

#67

A place must have
at least 10 residents to
qualify as a
"town."

ELSIE EILER IS THE MOST IMPORTANT RESIDENT OF MONOWI, NEBRASKA—AND THE ONLY ONE.

Elsie owns the only restaurant in town, and she runs for mayor every year. She's very active in campaigning and putting fliers on her business's windows. **Of course, she is the only person who votes, so she votes for herself and—surprise!—she wins.** When Elsie was growing up in Monowi, there were 150 people living in her town. But after World War II, farming conditions worsened and the economy suffered. Many people moved out of Monowi, and the rest passed away over time. Elsie's friends come from other parts of Nebraska to visit her restaurant.

Instant Genius

Monowi is a Native American word for "flower with milky juice."

Which sense is most closely connected to memory?

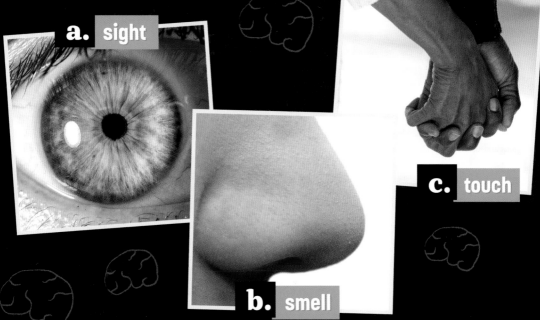

a. sight

b. smell

c. touch

ANSWER: **b** smell

PEOPLE CLOSELY ASSOCIATE SMELL WITH MEMORY AND EMOTION. WHY? The part of the brain that processes and recognizes different smells is right near the part of the brain that controls memories and emotions. This is why certain scents trigger specific memories. **The place where people process scents is called the olfactory bulb.** It goes from your nose to your brain. **It is connected to the hippocampus, which processes memories, and the amygdala, which processes emotions.** Scientists found that people have more brain activity when smelling something than they do when seeing the same object. **People also tend to smell in colors. In one demonstration, people were found to associate a grassy smell with green and brown, and citrus with yellow, orange, and green.**

Instant Genius
Smell is the only fully developed sense at birth.

Why do **turtles** have shells?

a. to protect their insides

b. because they never grew bones

c. to help them move faster

Slow and steady!

ANSWER: a | **to protect their insides**

MILLIONS OF YEARS AGO TURTLES HAD LARGE, HARD RIBS INSTEAD OF A SHELL. These large bones protected the turtle and helped it float in water. Over time, the ribs got wider and eventually joined together to form the outer shell they have today. Scientists think that turtle shells also evolved to help the turtle dig. With a heavy shell holding them down like an anchor, the turtles could use their strong front legs to dig with force. Digging was a way to uncover a cooler, safer environment in the hot, dry climates of southern Africa—where *Eunotosaurus,* an early turtle-like reptile, lived. Today, a shell's main job is to protect the turtle. If threatened, a turtle can pull itself into its shell. For most predators, the shell is too hard to eat or crush.

146

True or False:

Playing

is good
for your brain.

#70

NOW YOU KNOW!

Herring gulls have been observed in the wild playing catch with clams. They let them drop from their grip, then swoop down to snatch them again before the clams hit the ground.

ANSWER: True

PLAY IS IMPORTANT FOR BRAIN DEVELOPMENT. IT STIMULATES THE CONNECTIONS BETWEEN NERVE CELLS AND HELPS YOUR IMAGINATION GROW. By using your imagination more, you might be more creative as an adult. **Playing also builds physical and emotional strength. Physical play helps people develop motor skills such as running, coordination, and even writing.** There's a benefit in the classroom, too. Kids who play more have been found to do better on tests. Score!

Instant Genius

The Royal Game of Ur is the world's oldest board game, at 4,600 years old!

Which **primate** is most closely related to chimpanzees?

a. gorilla

b. human

c. orangutan

ANSWER: b human

WE SHARE 98.8 PERCENT OF OUR DNA WITH CHIMPS. HOW?
Humans and chimps had a common ancestor 6 or 7 million years ago. From there we developed differently. **Chimpanzees and humans belong to a larger group of mammals called primates. Gorillas and orangutans are also part of this group.** Primates are distinctly intelligent compared to other animals. Although 98.8 percent is a lot in common, the 1.2 percent difference is bigger than you might think. In fact, this small percentage in our genes equals about 35 million differences. Still, we share many similarities. **Chimpanzees smell, hear, feel, and see things a lot like we do.** Chimps can use tools, be playful, and express emotions, such as frowning when it rains.

#72

Water

always boils
at the same
temperature.

Instant Genius
Boiling water sometimes kills germs so it's safe to drink.

ANSWER: **False**

THE BOILING POINT OF WATER DEPENDS ON MANY FACTORS, INCLUDING ALTITUDE, ATMOSPHERIC PRESSURE, AND WHICH—IF ANY—CHEMICALS ARE IN THE WATER. **Water boils faster in higher altitudes, but it will take you longer to make pasta in the mountains than by the sea.** That's because air pressure decreases in higher altitudes. As a result, water boils at a lower temperature, so it takes your food longer to cook. What exactly is happening when you're waiting for your pasta water to bubble? When enough heat is applied, it moves around the molecules and causes them to break. **This is when they morph from a liquid into a gas, hence the bubbles floating to the water's surface.** Adding salt will make water boil faster, but not enough to really speed things up. **A heaping teaspoon will only increase the boiling point by four-hundredths of one degree—but you might like the flavor.**

How many **hairs** are on the average human head?

a. 1,000

b. 10,000

c. 100,000

ANSWER: C   100,000

THE AVERAGE PERSON'S HEAD HAS ABOUT 100,000 HAIRS. They grow from the thousands of pocket-like holes, called follicles, found on your skin. Follicles are responsible for growing hair all over the body, especially on the scalp. Each strand of hair grows for 3 to 7 years. **Then the follicle around the hair begins to shrink. After 2 to 4 months, the hair falls out completely, making way for new hair to grow in the follicle.** The hair that grows on all mammals is made from keratin, the same substance that makes up human fingernails and animal claws. **For most mammals, the hairs' main job is to insulate the body from the cold, making it easier to conserve body heat.**

Instant Genius
Hair covers roughly 90 percent of a human's skin.

What is the deepest lake on Earth?

a. Lake Baikal in Russia

c. Crater Lake in Oregon, U.S.A.

b. Lake Victoria in Tanzania and Uganda

Lake Baikal, Russia

ANSWER: a **Lake Baikal in Russia**

THE DEEPEST LAKE IN THE WORLD IS LAKE BAIKAL, IN THE RUSSIAN REGION OF SIBERIA. At 5,315 feet (1,620 m) deep, a 490-story building could fit inside it! **Lake Baikal is also the biggest freshwater lake, containing more than 20 percent of Earth's unfrozen freshwater.** It's so large that a water molecule would take 330 years to travel across it. How'd it get so big? **The lake—which is about 20 to 25 million years old—is located in an active continental rift zone, which gets about an inch (2.5 cm) wider every year.** As it widens, it also deepens. Below the water's surface are roughly 1,500 different types of animals, most of which can't be found anywhere else on Earth.

Who invented the cotton candy machine?

#75

a. a mathematician

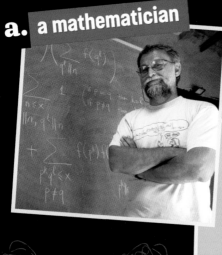

c. a dentist

b. a clown

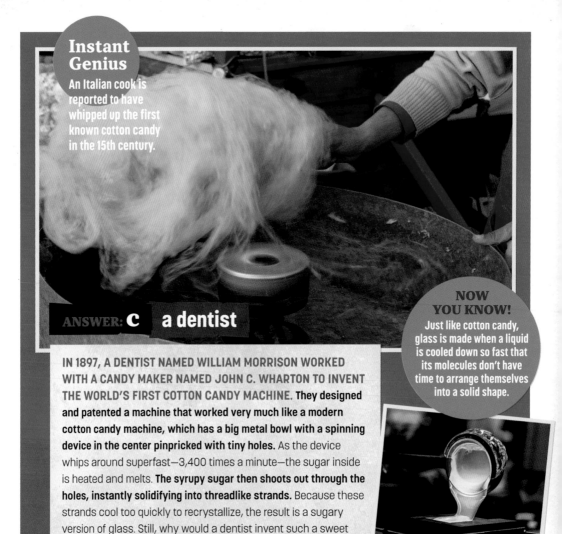

ANSWER: c a dentist

IN 1897, A DENTIST NAMED WILLIAM MORRISON WORKED WITH A CANDY MAKER NAMED JOHN C. WHARTON TO INVENT THE WORLD'S FIRST COTTON CANDY MACHINE. **They designed and patented a machine that worked very much like a modern cotton candy machine, which has a big metal bowl with a spinning device in the center pinpricked with tiny holes.** As the device whips around superfast—3,400 times a minute—the sugar inside is heated and melts. **The syrupy sugar then shoots out through the holes, instantly solidifying into threadlike strands.** Because these strands cool too quickly to recrystallize, the result is a sugary version of glass. Still, why would a dentist invent such a sweet treat? **Even though the sweet treat contains sugar, it's mostly air and is healthier than many other carnival treats.**

What do **cardinals** sometimes put all over their bodies?

a. flower petals

b. ants

c. honey

ANSWER: b ants

CARDINALS COVER THEMSELVES WITH ANTS, EITHER BY SITTING ON THEM OR RUBBING THEM ON THEIR FEATHERS. **This is called anting, and more than 200 bird species do it.** Scientists have a few ideas to explain this odd behavior. One explanation: The ants may serve as a natural insect repellent. **Ants have special acids in them that kill parasites, like mites and lice, on bird feathers.** Another reason may be that the crushed ants mimic the natural oils that birds produce, which can help soothe the area where new feathers are growing in. Anting also may be a way to remove natural toxins on the ants, so the birds can eat them. When ants aren't available, some bird species have found substitutions. **Birds have been seen "anting" with orange peels and mothballs too.**

Instant Genius
Most birds fly, but many can also swim, run, and jump.

True or False:

Fish
cough.

#77

Can I borrow somebody's elbow?

ANSWER: **True**

BOTH SALTWATER AND FRESHWATER FISH CAN COUGH—BUT IT'S A LITTLE DIFFERENT FROM HOW HUMANS COUGH. Instead of breathing air through lungs like humans do, fish use special organs called gills to take in water and filter out the oxygen they need to survive. If their gills are clogged with food particles, or they've been exposed to chemicals or toxins, they might cough in one of two ways. The first type is through the gills, when water enters the fish's mouth and passes over the gills with more force than usual, which blows out anything that's stuck in them. The second kind of cough happens when pressure builds up in the fish's gill covers. **Then water reverses direction across the gills, and debris is forced out through the mouth.**

Fish gills

Instant Genius
The gill covers on a fish are called opercula.

How are medicines made?

a. with human-made chemicals

b. with substances from nature

c. with both A and B

#78

Penicillin fungi

ANSWER: C **with both A and B**

Instant Genius

Some medicines are produced by extracting chemicals from crushed tree bark.

MEDICINES ARE MADE FROM BOTH HUMAN-MADE CHEMICALS AND SUBSTANCES FOUND IN NATURE. Antibiotics, such as those taken for strep throat, are made from natural bacteria. Labs grow the bacteria, then extract that ingredient from the bacteria. Other medicines, like the pain reliever ibuprofen, are the result of chemical reactions created in a lab. To create the medicines, different chemicals are either heated or cooled, then mixed together in a giant tank. Once the chemical reaction has taken place, the new concoction is superheated to boil off any excess chemicals. What remains is cooled into a powder that contains the medicine's active ingredient. The medicine is then pressed in tablets, transformed into a gel or cream, or bottled as a liquid ready to be packaged and sold in stores.

79

According to scientists, why do people participate in

dangerous sports?

a. to feel a thrill

b. to prove they are not afraid

c. to scare people

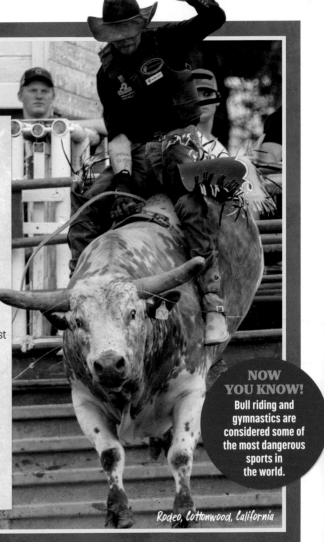

to feel a thrill

DIFFERENT PEOPLE HAVE DIFFERENT TOLERANCES FOR DOING RISKY ACTIVITIES. How do you measure that tolerance? **Scientists have created a sensation-seeking scale to determine how likely a person is to take part in risky adventures.** This test is broken down into four parts. The first two parts determine how much a person enjoys adventure and new experiences. The second two parts rate a person's impulsivity and tolerance for boredom. Sensation seekers lose interest in things easily and hate being bored. **When faced with a dangerous situation, their brains also tend to produce more dopamine, the neurotransmitter tied to pleasure, than in people who are less adventurous.** Daredevils also tend to produce less cortisol, the "stress hormone" that triggers your fight-or-flight response, than people who are less tolerant to risk.

NOW YOU KNOW!
Bull riding and gymnastics are considered some of the most dangerous sports in the world.

Rodeo, Cottonwood, California

How many flowers must **honeybees** visit to produce a pound (0.5 kg) of honey?

a. **200**

b. **2,000**

c. **2 million**

A swarm of bees sitting in a tree

NOW YOU KNOW!
Between 20,000 and 80,000 bees live in a single hive. The hive can weigh anywhere from 35 to 110 pounds (16 to 50 kg).

Instant Genius
Honeybees have four wings and five eyes.

ANSWER: C **2 million**

TO PRODUCE 1 POUND (0.5 KG) OF HONEY, HONEYBEES MUST TAP AN INCREDIBLE 2 MILLION FLOWERS. **Bees are about the size of a paper clip, yet their little bodies can fly at speeds up to 20 miles (32 km) an hour.** When honeybees leave their hives in search of nectar, they usually travel about a mile (1.6 km) away to find flowers. **In one trip alone, a honeybee can visit up to 100 flowers.** After a hard day's work, the honeybees come home to rest in their hive.

When the *Titanic* sank in 1912, how many dogs survived?

a. none

b. one

c. three

Though the *Titanic* set sail from England, it was constructed in Belfast, the capital city of what is now Northern Ireland.

TITANIC

TITANIC DISASTER GREAT LOSS OF LIFE
EVENING NEWS

Instant Genius

The *Titanic* took more than two and a half hours to sink.

ANSWER: c **three**

ON APRIL 15, 1912, THE RMS *TITANIC*—THE LARGEST SHIP TO EVER SAIL AT THE TIME—STRUCK AN ICEBERG AND SANK INTO THE ICY WATERS OF THE NORTH ATLANTIC. **Of the 2,224 people on board, more than 1,500 died.** Many animals, including dogs, cats, birds, and rats, were also aboard the ship. Surprisingly, three of these dogs survived. **All three pets were very small and had owners traveling in first class.** As the ship was sinking, two Pomeranians and a Pekingese were sneaked on board lifeboats with their owners. **The *Titanic* should have had 48 lifeboats—enough to hold all passengers—but it departed on its voyage with only 20.** The ship's owners did this on purpose because they thought more lifeboats would have crowded the deck and led people to think the ship was unsafe.

Tigers

have striped skin.

#82

NOW YOU KNOW!
Tigers have a patch of white fur on each ear, which mimics another set of eyes. Scientists think the spots may scare away other animals by making them think they are being watched.

ANSWER: True

JUST LIKE HUMAN FINGERPRINTS, NO TWO TIGERS HAVE THE SAME STRIPES. **What all tigers do have in common, though, is striped skin beneath their fur.** If you were to shave a tiger's fur, you'd see the same dark pattern of stripes on its skin. This is probably because of the deeply rooted hair follicles embedded in the tiger's skin. **This is similar to the way some men get beard stubble known as the "five o'clock shadow."** The thickness of a tiger's coat can vary. In cold areas, tiger coats grow more densely to keep them warm. In warmer climates, a tiger's coat is thinner with shorter fur, allowing more heat to escape through the skin.

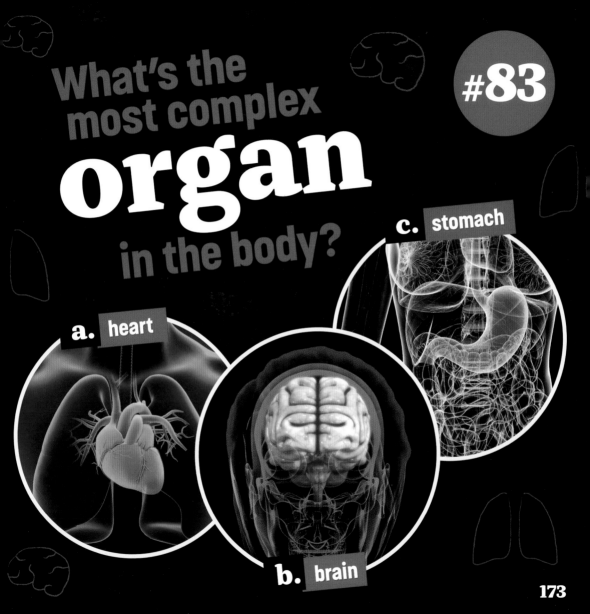

What's the most complex **organ** in the body?

#83

a. heart

b. brain

c. stomach

173

AS YOU PONDERED THE ANSWER, YOU WERE PUTTING THIS ORGAN TO GOOD USE: THE BRAIN!
Your brain juggles a lot of responsibilities—it's where all your thoughts, actions, feelings, memories, and life experiences are created. An army of approximately 86 billion active neurons does this complicated work. **Cells called glia protect these neurons and keep the brain healthy.** Hundreds of billions of brain cells are interlinked through trillions of connections. **Neurons work with one another as a team, communicating information in a circuit.** When they communicate correctly, you have a functioning nervous system. No, the brain doesn't control how nervous you might feel before a big test, but it does control functions like your heart rate and breathing, which might speed up when you get a little anxious! **It commands other systems in the body too, such as those that help your glands work properly and those that ward off bacteria and viruses.**

NOW YOU KNOW!
An adult brain weighs about 3 pounds (1.4 kg) and is composed of fat and protein.

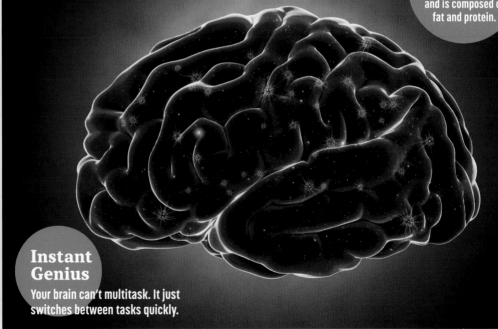

Instant Genius
Your brain can't multitask. It just switches between tasks quickly.

What has been banned from Antarctica?

#84

a. dogs

b. boats

c. scientists

NOW
YOU KNOW!
By sleeping near people to keep them warm, dogs in Antarctica have saved people from hypothermia and death.

ANSWER: **a** **dogs**

THE BAN ON DOGS, IMPOSED IN 1994 BY THE PROTOCOL ON ENVIRONMENTAL PROTECTION AS A CLAUSE TO THE ANTARCTIC TREATY, WAS DUE TO THE FEAR OF DOGS SPREADING DISEASES TO SEALS. There was also the concern that off-leash dogs might disturb wildlife. Before the ban, sled dogs were a big part of life in Antarctica. Explorer Roald Amundsen used sled dogs to reach the South Pole for the first time in 1911. **Huskies, a popular breed of sled dog, are large with thick coats of straight fur to keep them warm. Huskies are very strong and can carry lots of supplies on their sleds—still used in the Arctic.** Teams of 12 dogs pull the sleds, with the strongest at the back. **These packs of dogs can drag sleds that weigh up to 1,200 pounds (544 kg).**

Only female animals give birth.

Instant Genius

Seahorses can carry up to 2,000 babies, called fry, at once.

85

ANSWER: False

SEAHORSES, PIPEFISH, AND SEA DRAGONS ARE ALL PART OF A FAMILY OF FISH IN WHICH THE MALES CAN GIVE BIRTH. After mating, the female seahorse deposits her eggs into a special organ on the male's belly, called a **brood pouch.** Over the next 10 to 25 days, the eggs grow and develop—and eventually hatch—inside the pouch, where they receive all the nutrition they need. When it's time to give birth, the male's abdomen opens and, through a small hole, he pushes out all the babies very quickly in a rapid motion. **Seahorses are the only animals known to give birth this way. Male pipefish and sea dragons instead carry eggs under their tails.**

NOW YOU KNOW!

Seahorses range in size from as small as a grain of rice to more than a foot (0.3 m) long. The largest, the big-bellied seahorse, lives off the coast of Australia and New Zealand.

Why do
professional
swimmers
and cyclists
sometimes

#86

shave their legs?

a. to look sleek

b. to make them faster

c. to follow the rules

Instant Genius

Drag is stronger in water than in air because water is denser.

ANSWER: b **to make them faster**

PROFESSIONAL SWIMMERS AND CYCLISTS SHAVE OFF BODY HAIR TO REDUCE DRAG, OR THE FORCE THAT SLOWS DOWN OBJECTS IN MOTION, MAKING IT HARDER FOR THEM TO MOVE FORWARD. For example, water pushes against swimmers as they swim. **Athletes must spend extra energy overcoming the drag force that's resisting their movement.** Without extra hair, the body is smoother and therefore can glide through the water with less drag. The same is true for cyclists. **Shaving reduces drag in the air. One study found that shaving reduced drag by 7 percent.**

87

Who invented
meteorology?

a. Aristotle

c. Benjamin Franklin

b. Leonardo da Vinci

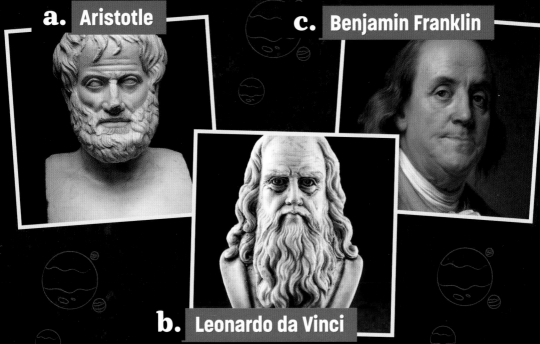

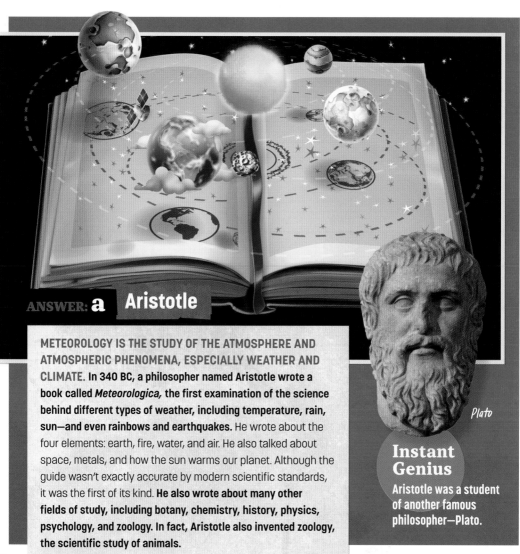

ANSWER: a **Aristotle**

METEOROLOGY IS THE STUDY OF THE ATMOSPHERE AND ATMOSPHERIC PHENOMENA, ESPECIALLY WEATHER AND CLIMATE. In 340 BC, a philosopher named Aristotle wrote a book called *Meteorologica,* the first examination of the science behind different types of weather, including temperature, rain, sun—and even rainbows and earthquakes. He wrote about the four elements: earth, fire, water, and air. He also talked about space, metals, and how the sun warms our planet. Although the guide wasn't exactly accurate by modern scientific standards, it was the first of its kind. **He also wrote about many other fields of study, including botany, chemistry, history, physics, psychology, and zoology. In fact, Aristotle also invented zoology, the scientific study of animals.**

Plato

Instant Genius

Aristotle was a student of another famous philosopher—Plato.

#88

Anyone else hot?

True or False:

Cats
sweat.

ANSWER: **True**

CATS DON'T FREQUENTLY PANT LIKE DOGS DO. INSTEAD, CATS COPE WITH HEAT BY SWEATING THROUGH THEIR PAWS. On especially hot days, cats may even leave wet footprints. **A cat's paws aren't big enough to offer a lot of relief from the heat, however, so they also seek ways to avoid overheating in the first place.** Cats will look for shady spots and lie down to keep themselves cool. Cats also constantly groom themselves to cool off. This method works the same way our sweat does. When their saliva evaporates from their fur, it decreases their body temperature. When cats pant, they do it as a last resort. **This means they are in danger of overheating, and they need to reach a cooler temperature.**

What is a large **raindrop** shape liked?

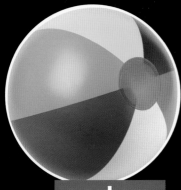

a. a sphere

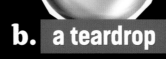

b. a teardrop

c. a hamburger bun

Phantom rain clouds

NOW YOU KNOW!
Phantom rain falls from clouds but never touches Earth. It evaporates along the way.

ANSWER: C   a hamburger bun

IT'S A MYTH THAT A DROP OF RAIN IS SHAPED LIKE A TEARDROP. **A large raindrop is actually shaped like the top of a hamburger bun!** How does nature cook these up? Tiny raindrops are shaped like spheres. Larger raindrops fall with greater velocity than smaller sphere-shaped ones. **As they plummet toward Earth, air pushes up against the raindrops. The surface tension of the water droplet pushes back, and the two forces work against each other, causing the droplet to flatten at the bottom and grow wider.** When the raindrop gets big enough, the air pressure overpowers the surface tension holding the drop together, and the drop starts splitting into two.

90

True or False:

Alligators
prey on manatees.

I see something tasty!

An alligator consuming a large fish

ANSWER: False

ALLIGATORS ARE OPPORTUNISTIC FEEDERS, WHICH MEANS THEY EAT A VARIETY OF ANIMALS THAT CROSS THEIR PATH. The diet of these large reptiles includes turtles, snakes, small mammals, fish, and even—gulp—smaller alligators. Instead of munching on manatees, though, alligators let them swim by. Why? First of all, manatees are large and have thick hides, which are hard to chew through. **They are also fast swimmers, and they can hold their breath underwater for more than 20 minutes.** That's four times longer than alligators, which need to surface every 3 to 5 minutes to breathe. **So when a manatee wants to pass an alligator in its path, it simply gives the alligator a nudge.**

Instant Genius

Manatees have been mistaken for mermaids.

91

What is
heterochromia?

a. the fear of rainbows

c. a rare type of birthmark

b. a condition causing different-colored eyes

Instant Genius
No two people have the exact same eye color.

ANSWER: b a condition causing different-colored eyes

NOW YOU KNOW!
Complete heterochromia is rare in humans, affecting fewer than 200,000 people in the United States. It is much more common in dogs, cats, and horses.

HETEROCHROMIA IS A CONDITION CAUSING TWO DIFFERENT-COLORED IRISES, THE COLORED PART OF THE EYE. **Complete heterochromia is when two irises are completely different colors, such as one blue and one green.** Partial heterochromia is when one part of the iris is a different color from the rest of it. Central heterochromia is when there is a ring around the iris with a different color. What causes it? **Eye color is determined by pigment called melanin.** If you have less melanin in your eyes, they are lighter in color, and if you have more, they are darker. **Genetics control the amount of melanin in the iris.** If you have heterochromia, the amount of melanin in your eyes varies. **Usually people are born with the condition, but sometimes an illness, medicine, or injury can cause it.**

Why do **wildebeests** migrate?

a. to find food and water   **b.** to stay warm

c. to avoid predators

IN ONE OF THE GREATEST SPECTACLES OF THE NATURAL WORLD, AFRICAN ANTELOPES CALLED WILDEBEESTS MIGRATE ACROSS THE SERENGETI AT THE END OF THE RAINY SEASON TO FIND FOOD AND WATER IN OTHER PLACES. **They have been taking the same route for more than 2 million years!** For the first half of the year, wildebeests live in Tanzania, where they give birth. By migration time in May or June, the young wildebeests are old enough to keep up with the rest of the herd. **More than 1.5 million wildebeests set off on the journey north toward the Masai Mara National Reserve in Kenya.** Along the way, they cross treacherous crocodile-infested waters and survive stampedes, which occur when a large group of animals is startled and tries to rush to safety.

Instant Genius
A group of wildebeests is called a confusion.

Wildebeest migration, Masai Mara, Kenya

NOW YOU KNOW!
Zebras, gazelles, and impalas take part in the migration, too. As they move, zebras chomp on the Serengeti's fresh grasses.

True or False:

You can walk to **Russia** from the **United States.**

#93

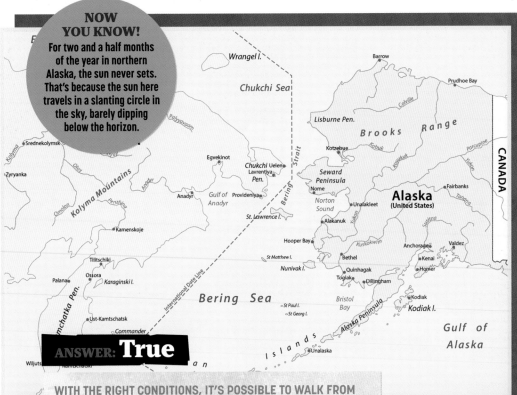

Wrangel I.

Chukchi Sea

Barrow

Prudhoe Bay

Colville

Lisburne Pen.

Brooks Range

Kotzebue

Kobuk

Koyukuk

Parcupine

Yukon

CANADA

Palyavaam

Kolyma

Srednekolymsk

Zyryanka

Kolyma Mountains

Oloy

Anadyr

Omolon

Penzhina

Kamenskoje

Tilitschiki

Ossora

Palana

Karaginski I.

Ust-Kamtschatsk

Commander

Wiljuts

Kamtschatski

Egvekinot

Chukchi
Lavrentiya
Pen.

Uelen

Bering Strait

Gulf of
Anadyr

Providyeniya

St. Lawrence I.

Seward
Peninsula

Nome

Norton
Sound

Unalakleet

Yukon

Alaska
(United States)

Fairbanks

Tanana

Hooper Bay

St Matthew I.

Nunivak I.

Bethel

Kuskokwim

Anchorage

Kenai

Valdez

Susitna

Quinhagak

Toglak

Dillingham

Homer

St Paul I.

St Georg I.

Bristol
Bay

Alaska Peninsula

Kodiak

Kodiak I.

Bering Sea

Alakanuk

Gulf of
Alaska

Islands

Unalaska

International Date Line

ANSWER: True

WITH THE RIGHT CONDITIONS, IT'S POSSIBLE TO WALK FROM THE UNITED STATES TO RUSSIA. You'd have to start in the state of Alaska, U.S.A., which is not attached to the continental United States but actually borders western Canada. **From its farthest western point, Alaska is separated from Russia by the Bering Strait, a body of water about 55 miles (89 km) wide at its narrowest point.** Two islands lie in the middle of the strait: Big Diomede, which Russia owns, and Little Diomede, which the United States owns. **So in winter, when the 2.5 miles (4 km) of water that separate the two islands freezes, you could walk from one country to the other.**

Instant Genius
In 1959, Alaska became the 49th U.S. state.

How much food can an **adult's stomach** hold?

a. 1 pint (473 ml)

b. 1 quart (0.95 L)

c. 1 gallon (3.8 L)

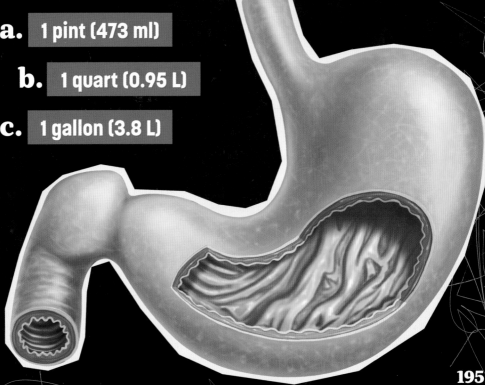

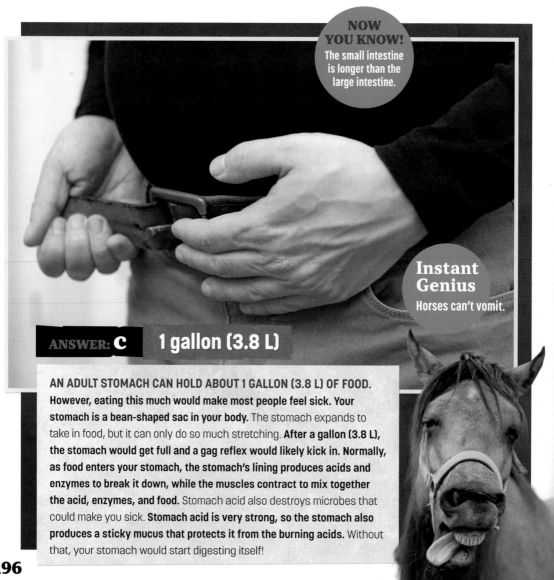

Instant Genius
Horses can't vomit.

ANSWER: C 1 gallon (3.8 L)

AN ADULT STOMACH CAN HOLD ABOUT 1 GALLON (3.8 L) OF FOOD. However, eating this much would make most people feel sick. Your stomach is a bean-shaped sac in your body. The stomach expands to take in food, but it can only do so much stretching. **After a gallon (3.8 L), the stomach would get full and a gag reflex would likely kick in.** Normally, as food enters your stomach, the stomach's lining produces acids and enzymes to break it down, while the muscles contract to mix together the acid, enzymes, and food. Stomach acid also destroys microbes that could make you sick. **Stomach acid is very strong, so the stomach also produces a sticky mucus that protects it from the burning acids.** Without that, your stomach would start digesting itself!

#95

Which of these was true about

Coco Chanel?

a. She grew up in an orphanage.

b. She invented the "little black dress."

c. Both A and B

Coco Chanel, London, England

ANSWER: C **Both A and B**

THIS FRENCH FASHION ICON WAS BORN IN 1883 AND DIED IN 1971. Her family was poor. When she was 12 years old, her mother died and her father left her at an orphanage, where she learned to sew. **At the age of 18, Chanel started sewing her own clothes.** Fashion at that time was fancy and expensive. **Chanel rebelled against that and designed a style that was the opposite: simple and elegant.** Because of her childhood as a poor orphan, Chanel wanted her clothes to be accessible to everyone. **The original little black dress, which debuted in the 1920s, was affordable during the Great Depression, when people didn't have a lot of money to spend on clothes.** It could be worn in different styles, with various accessories, and for different occasions. The idea of the little black dress is still popular today.

Instant Genius

The "little black dress" is often nicknamed the "LBD."

How long is one year on Uranus?

a. 45 Earth years

b. 84 Earth years

c. 92 Earth years

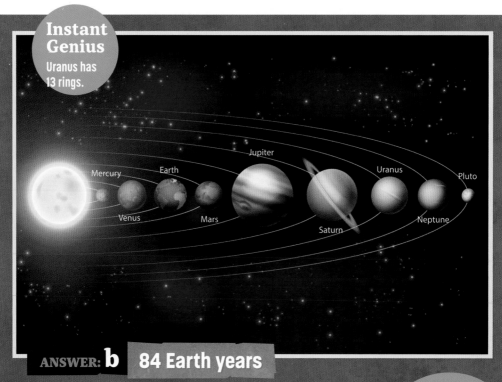

Instant
Genius
Uranus has
13 rings.

Mercury
Venus
Earth
Mars
Jupiter
Saturn
Uranus
Neptune
Pluto

ANSWER: b **84 Earth years**

ONE YEAR ON URANUS IS EQUIVALENT TO 84 YEARS ON EARTH.
This means that it takes 84 Earth years for Uranus to orbit the sun once. Why is Uranus so slow? Compared to Earth, Uranus is much farther away from the sun, so it takes longer to make a full circle around it. **Uranus has four seasons a year, just like Earth.** Each season, however, lasts 21 years! **In winter there is absolutely no sunlight, and during summer there's light all day and night. No matter the season, the temperature on Uranus is cold, because the planet is so far from the sun.**

NOW YOU KNOW!
Uranus is tilted at a 98-degree angle. Scientists think that's because some earthlike mass bonked into Uranus and knocked it over during the formation of the solar system.

What happens to your
hair strands
as you age?

a. **They get thinner.**

b. **They get thicker.**

c. **They remain the same.**

A close-up photo of human hair taken under a microscope

ANSWER: a **They get thinner.**

AS HUMANS AGE, THE STRANDS OF HAIR ON THEIR HEAD GET THINNER. A single hair usually stays on the body for two to seven years. Each strand of hair falls out and is replaced with a new one. **How much hair you start with when you are young depends on the genes you inherited from your parents.** As you get older, your hair grows back more slowly. **The hair also loses pigment, which is what gives hair its color. When this happens, it turns gray or white.** Often, as you age, the body stops making more hair to replace the hair that falls out, so your hair gets thinner. **Facial and body hair gets thinner, too. But facial hair in places like ears, noses, and eyebrows may grow even more!**

Instant Genius

Hair and fingernails are made of protein.

#98

How do **pigs** protect their skin from the sun?

a. They stand in the shade.

b. They don't need to; they don't get sunburned.

c. They use mud as sunscreen.

203

They use mud as sunscreen.

PIGS ROLL AROUND TO COVER THEMSELVES WITH A SPECIAL SUNSCREEN—MUD! Pigs need sun protection because the sun's harsh UV rays can damage their skin. When sunburned, pigskin gets red and splotchy and painful to the touch—just like a human's skin might. **Pigs also roll in the mud to keep themselves cool, especially in hot temperatures.** How? The water in mud evaporates more slowly than water alone. And pigs aren't the only animals to use mud as sunscreen—rhinos and hippos also bathe in mud to protect their hides from the sun. **Mud also helps lower the pigs' body temperatures on warm days and keeps insects away.**

Instant Genius
Piglets can learn to recognize their names by three weeks.

Human teeth

are as strong as shark teeth.

#99

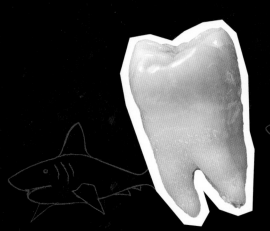

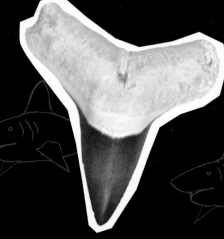

A kitefin shark's jaws and teeth

NOW YOU KNOW!
Unlike humans, who only get two sets of teeth, sharks lose and grow teeth continuously throughout their lives. A shark's teeth grow much faster than human teeth do.

Instant Genius
Scientists estimate that sharks first appeared 455 million years ago.

ANSWER: **True**

HUMAN TEETH ARE AS STRONG AS SHARK TEETH. **Scientists compared the enamel-like coatings of shark teeth to the enamel on human wisdom teeth.** Although the two types of tooth coating contained different minerals, they are equally tough. This is because the outside of human teeth is made up of both minerals and proteins, a combination that keeps the surface from shattering under sudden impact. Sharks definitely have some advantages when it comes to their teeth, though. **Sharks' teeth are made of fluoride, so they don't need to worry about getting cavities.** And unlike humans, sharks are born with teeth. They have a lot more, too! **Humans have one row of teeth, but sharks normally have between 5 and 15 rows. One species of shark, the bull shark, has 50 rows of teeth!**

100

What does a

black hole

do to a passing star?

a. repels it

b. sucks it in

c. explodes it

The supermassive black hole at the center of the Milky Way galaxy is called Sagittarius A, and it has a mass of about 4 million suns.

Instant Genius

Black holes are invisible, so scientists study the stars around them to pinpoint their locations.

ANSWER: **b** **sucks it in**

BLACK HOLES ARE PLACES IN SPACE WHERE THE GRAVITY IS SO STRONG THAT EVEN LIGHT CAN'T ESCAPE THEIR PULL. **The extreme gravitational pull is due to a massive amount of matter getting squeezed into a tiny space.** This causes a vacuum that sucks in everything around it. **Black holes can be created in the aftermath of a dying star.** Black holes can be as small as atoms or as large as stars. **Stellar black holes can be more than 20 times the mass of the sun.** But these aren't even the largest black holes. The largest black holes are called supermassive black holes, and they have as much mass as 1 million suns put together. **Scientists think that every large galaxy, including our own, contains a supermassive black hole at its center.**

A dog's nose

is about how many times more sensitive than a human's nose?

a. 10 times

c. 100,000 times

b. 100 times

Sniffing all day makes me tired!

ANSWER: C

100,000 times more sensitive

DOGS' NOSES ARE 100,000 TIMES MORE SENSITIVE THAN HUMAN NOSES—AT LEAST! Some scientists think they may be even more sensitive. **The cells that allow humans and animals to smell are called "olfactory receptors," and dogs have a lot more of them than humans do.** Dogs use their keen sense of smell to detect prey and danger in the wild. **Humans have also taken advantage of this canine superpower to assist police, military personnel, and first responders.** Dogs' mighty noses can sniff out illegal substances, explosives, and even people. **Some dogs can even be trained to sniff out certain types of cancer and other diseases, and to alert a person with epilepsy that a seizure is about to happen.**

Instant Genius
African elephants have the best sense of smell in the animal world.

Turn to page 215 for the answers!

Index

Page numbers in *italic* refer to images.

A

amphibians. *See also* animals.
glass frogs 127–128, *127, 128*
Meganeuropsis and 108
animals. *See also* amphibians; birds; cats; dogs;
insects; marine life; reptiles.
beavers 95–96, *95, 96*
bull riding 166, *166*
chimpanzees 149–150, *150*
cows 17–18, *17*
elephants 11–12, *11*, 57–58, *57*, 210, *210*
hair 154, *154*, 172, *172*
horses 190, 196, *196*
Japanese macaques 10, *10*
kangaroo rats 12, *12*
llamas 63–64, *63, 64*
Megalonyx sloths 96, *96*
naked mole rats 83–84, *83, 84*
pigs 203–204, *203, 204*
polar bears 34, *34*
primates 149–150, *149, 150*
raccoons 94, *94*
rhinos 12, *12*, 204
rodents 83–84, *83, 84*, 95–96
sloths 48, *48*, 96, *96*
tigers 171–172, *171, 172*
wildebeests 191–192, *191, 192*
zoology 182

B

birds. *See also* animals.
anting 159–160, *159, 160*
bones *99*, 100
cardinals 159–160, *160*
feathers *99*, 100, *100*, 160
herring gulls 148, *148*
hummingbirds 22, 31–32, *31, 32*, 100
pigeons 99–100, *99, 100*
tetrachromacy 31–32
body
antibiotics 164, *164*
blood 38, *38*, 52, 62, 88, 106, *106*
blood vessels *38*, 105–106, *105*
bones 37–38, *37, 38*, 47–48, *47, 48*,
59–60, *59, 60*, 125–126, *125, 126*
brain 19–20, 76, 102, 126, 144, 147–148, 166,
173–174, *173, 174*
breathing 48, 66, *66*, 174

cartilage 48, 90
cells 20, 38, 52, 64, 88, 106, *106*, 148,
174, 210
COVID-19 63–64, *64*
cryotherapy 51–52, *51, 52*
ears 46, 90, 202
eyes 20, 32, 76, 189–190, *189, 190*
fingernails 100, 154, 202
hair 100, 153–154, *153, 154*, 179–180,
179, 201–202, *201, 202*
happiness 76, 101–102, *101, 102*
heterochromia 189–190, *189, 190*
intestines 196
lactose intolerance 17–18, *18*
legs 179–180, *179*
liver 87–88, *87, 88*
lungs 48, 162
mandibles 126, *126*
medicines 163–164, *163*, 190
memory 143–144
muscles 46, 75–76, *76*, 98, 134, 196
nerve cells 20, 148
olfactory receptors 144, 210
organs 38, 48, 87–88, *87, 88*
play 147–148, *147, 148*
ribs 47–48, *47, 48*
sense of sight 32, 144, 150
sense of smell 143–144, *143, 144*, 150, 210
skin 76, 88, *88*, 154, *154*
skull 60, *60*, 125–126, *125, 126*
sleep 19–20, *19, 20*, 102, 176
smiling 75–76, *75, 76*
stomach 195–196, *195, 196*
teeth 126, 205–206, *205*
water 37–38

C

cats. *See also* animals.
cucumbers and 23–24, *24*
heterochromia 190, *190*
sweating 183–184
vocal cords 93–94
whiskers 53–54, *53, 54*

D

dogs. *See also* animals.
Antarctica and 175–176, *176*
communication 140, *140*
heterochromia 190
huskies 176
kicking 139–140, *140*
Labrador retrievers 62, *62*
panting 184, *184*
population 61–62, *62*
puppies 45–46, *45, 46*
sense of hearing 45–46, *46*
sense of sight 46, *46*
sense of smell 117–118, *117, 118*, 140,
209–210, *210*

sled dogs 176
Titanic survivors 169–170, *170*

E

Earth. *See also* geography; landmarks.
atmosphere 86, *86*, 108, 120, 182
avalanches 129–130, *130*
islands 33–34, *33, 34*, 156, 194
volcanoes 80, *80*
elements
mercury 30, 104, *104*
metals 30, 103–104, *103, 104*, 182
periodic table 30, *30*, 104
solar system and 29–30

F

foods
cow's milk 17–18, *17, 18*
Disgusting Food Museum 15–16, *16*
salt 29–30, *29*, 152

G

geography. *See also* Earth; landmarks.
Africa 59–60, 146, 192, *192*
Alaska 194, *194*
Andes Mountains 68, *68*, 79–80, *79, 80*
Antarctica 40, 175–176
Aomori City, Japan 112
Bering Strait 194, *194*
Canada *8–9*, 9–10, *10*, 34, 132, 194, *194*
Chile 79–80, *79, 80*
Colorado 120, 130
Greenland 33–34, *33, 34*
Lake Baikal 155–156, *155, 156*
Monowi, Nebraska 142, *142*
Peru 67–68, *67, 68*, 80, 130
Point Nemo 39–40, *39, 40*
Russia *130*, 155–156, *155, 156*,
193–194, *194*
Shkhara Mountains *130*
Sweden 15–16, *15*
Tokyo, Japan 25–26, *25*
towns 141–142, *142*
United States 61–62, *61, 62*, 74, *74*,
193–194, *194*

H

history
Abraham Lincoln 132, *132*
Ada Lovelace 123–124, *124*
Alexander Graham Bell 135–136, *135, 136*
ancient Egypt *17*, 52, 148, *148*
Aristotle 181–182, *181*
Coco Chanel 197–198, *197, 198*
Cradle of Humankind 59–60, *60*
fossils 60, *60*, 90, 96, 108
Inca people 68, *68*
Machu Picchu 67–68, *67, 68*
pirates 82, *82*
Plato 182, *182*

Roald Amundsen 176
Royal Game of Ur 148, *148*
Titanic 169–170, *170*
Yuri Gagarin 114

I

insects. *See also* animals.
  ants 159–160, *159, 160*
  cockroaches 116, *116*
  dragonflies 108, *108*
  froghoppers 77–78, *77, 78*
  honeybees 167–168, *167, 168*
  Meganeuropsis 107–108, *107, 108*
  praying mantids 21–22, *21, 22*
  spiders 35–36, *35, 36*
  spittlebugs 77–78, *77, 78*
  stereopsis 21–22
  wasps 128

L

landmarks. *See also* Earth; geography.
  Champs-Élysées 42, *42*
  Machu Picchu 67–68, *67, 68*
  New Seven Wonders of the World
    67–68, *67, 68*

M

marine life. *See also* animals.
  alligators 187–188, *187, 188*
  births by males 177–178
  bones of 89–90, 126, *126*, 146
  brood pouches 178
  coughing 161–162
  countershading 58
  crocodiles 69–70, *69, 70*, 192
  dolphins 57–58, *57, 58*, 121–122, *121, 122*
  gills 162, *162*
  manatees 187–188, *188*
  nerpa seals 156, *156*
  opercula 162
  orcas 122, *122*
  oysters 109–110, *109, 110*
  seahorses 178, *178*
  sharks 16, 70, 89–90, *89, 90*, 205–206, *206*
  squid 58, *58*, 66, 137–138, *138*
  triggerfish 110, *110*
  turtles 145–146, *145, 146*, 188
  whales 48, 65–66, *65, 66*, 70, 122, 138, *138*
money
  coins 43–44, *43, 44*
  Great Depression 198

P

plants
  cherry blossoms 26, *26*
  cucumbers 23–24, *24*
  flowers 24, 26, *26*, 167–168, *167*
  hygrometers 55–56

medicines and 164, *164*
pinecones 55–56, *55, 56*

R

reptiles. *See also* animals.
  alligators 187–188, *187, 188*
  crocodiles 69–70, *69, 70*, 192
  dinosaurs 32, *32*, 146
  snakes 24, *24*, 84, 188
  tetrachromacy 32
  turtles 145–146, *145, 146*, 188

S

sounds
  "The Bloop" 40
  Mars 71–72, *71*
  vocal cords 93–94
  yodeling 129–130, *129*
space
  Andromeda galaxy 91–92, *91, 92*
  astronauts 14, *14*, 28, *28*, 40, *50*, 113–114, *114*
  black holes 207–208, *207, 208*
  constellations 92, *92*
  cosmonauts 114, *114*
  elements in 29–30, *30*
  gravity 28, 50, 72, 207–208
  International Space Station 13–14, *13, 14*, 40, *50*
  liquids in 49–50, *49, 50*
  Mars 14, 71–72, *71*
  salt 29–30, *29*
  solar system 30, 200, *200*
  spacecraft 40, 72, *72*
  stars 30, 92, *92*, 114, 207–208, *207*
  Uranus 199–200, *199, 200*
  Vomit Comet 27–28, *28*
sports
  auto racing 133–134, *133, 134*
  bull riding 166, *166*
  cycling 41–42, *41, 42*, 179–180, *180*
  danger and 165–166, *165, 166*
  gymnastics 116, 166
  running 97–98, *97, 98*, 148
  snowball fights *8–9*, 9–10
  snowmobiling 130, *130*
  spectators 115–116, *115, 116*
  swimming 179–180, 180

T

technology
  computers 123–124, *123*
  cotton candy machines 157–158, *158*
  cryotherapy 51–52, *51, 52*
  hydrophones 40
  International Space Station 13–14, *13, 14*, 40, *50*
  Mars InSight lander 72, *72*
  motors 81–82
  telephones 135–136, *136*

temperatures
  Aristotle and 182
  body hair and 154
  boiling point of water 151–152, *151*
  cotton candy 158, *158*
  exothermic insects 78
  gaseous metals 103–104
  glass 158, *158*
  liver and 88
  pigs and 204
  snow 112
  sweating 184
  Uranus 200
transportation
  cars 73–74, *73, 74*, 133–134, *133, 134*
  Titanic 169–170, *170*
  Tokyo, Japan 26
  trains 26, 131–132, *131, 132*
  tugboats 81–82, *81, 82*
  Vomit Comet 27–28, *28*

W

water
  Bering Strait 194, *194*
  "The Bloop" 40
  boiling point 151–152, *151*
  bones 37–38
  clouds 85–86, *85, 86*, 186, *186*
  countershading 58
  drag 180
  hailstones 119–120, *120*
  hygrometers 55–56
  islands 33–34, *33, 34*, 156, 194
  Lake Baikal 155–156, *156*
  migration and 192
  mud 204
  polar regions 121–122
  snow *8–9*, 9–10, 112, 130, *130*
  sounds of 40, 72
  space and 49–50, *49, 50*
  spittlebugs 78
  surface tension 50, 186
  tubers 84
weather
  avalanches 129–130, *130*
  clouds 85–86, *85, 86*, 186, *186*
  global warming and 34, 86
  hailstones 119–120, *120*
  hygrometers 55–56
  meteorology 181–182
  pinecones and 55–56, *55, 56*
  rain 132, 182, 185–186, *186*
  snow *8–9*, 9–10, *10*, 52, 111–112, *111, 112*, 129–130, *130*, 132
  supercell thunderstorms 120

213

Photo Credits

The publishers would like to thank the following for the use of their images. While every effort has been made to credit images, the publishers will be pleased to correct any errors or omissions in future editions of the book.

t = top; b = bottom; l = left; r = right; c = center

123rf.com: p. 126(tr).

Alamy: pp. 10(cl), 12(t), 17, 22(br), 24(t), 28(t,cr), 41, 60, 62(t), 64(t), 65, 70, 73(cr), 74(t,cr), 88(t), 92(cr), 97, 98, 108(t), 113(cr), 124(l), 126(tl,br), 132(cr), 135(bc), 142, 148(t,br), 150(br), 156(br), 157(bc), 170(cl), 178(t), 186, 197, 198(t,cl), 202.

Dreamstime: pp. 1, 2(l,br), 4, 5, 7, 8–9, 9(cl,cr,bc), 11, 12(bl), 13, 15(cl,c,br), 16(t,bl), 18(t,br), 19(c,bl,br), 20, 21, 22(t), 23, 24(br), 25(c,bl,br), 26(t,br), 27(c,bl,br), 29, 30(tl,t), 31, 32(t,br), 33(cr,bl,bc), 34(t,br), 35, 36(t,br), 37, 38, 39(c,bl,br), 42(tr), 43, 44(t,br), 45, 46t,br), 47, 48(t,bl), 49, 51(cl,cr,bc), 52(l,br), 53, 54, 55, 56(t,br), 57(bl,br), 59(cl,cr,bc), 61(cl,cr,bc), 62(br), 63, 64(Covid virus), 66(br), 67(cr,bl,br), 68, 69, 71, 73(cl,bc), 75, 76(t,br), 77, 78(t), 79(cr,bl,br), 80, 81, 82(t,br), 83(cl,cr,bc), 85, 86, 87(cr,bl,br), 88(cr), 89, 90(t), 91(cr), 92(t), 93, 94(t,br), 95(bl,br), 96(t), 99(cl,cr,bc), 100(t,br), 101, 102, 103, 104(t,br), 106(t,cr), 107(cl,cr,bc), 109, 110(t,br), 111, 112, 113(cl,bc), 114(t,bl), 115, 116(t,br), 117, 118(t,bl), 119(cl,cr,bc), 120, 121, 122, 123(cl,cr,bc), 124(br), 125, 127, 128(br), 129, 130(t,cr), 131, 132(t), 133, 134(t,bl), 136(bl), 137(cl,cr,bc), 138, 139(cl,c,br), 140(br), 141, 143(cl,cr,bc), 144, 145, 146(t,br), 147, 149(cl,c,cr), 150(t), 151, 152, 153, 154(t,cr), 155(cl,cr,bc), 156(t), 157(cl,cr), 158(t,br), 159(cl,cr,bc), 160(t,br,ants), 161, 162(t,cr), 163, 164(t,bl), 165, 166, 167, 168(t,br), 169, 170(t), 171, 172, 173(cr,bl,bc), 174, 175(cl,bl,br), 176(t,br), 177, 179, 180(t,cr), 181(cl,bc), 182(t), 183, 184 (t,br), 185(cl,cr,bc), 187, 188(t,cl), 189(cl,cr,bc), 190(t,br), 191, 192, 193, 194, 195, 196(t,br), 199, 200, 201, 203, 204, 205(bl,br), 206(br), 207, 209, 210(t,br), 211(t,b), 215.

Getty Images: p. 42(t).

iStockphoto: pp. 66(t), 90(br), 105.

Werner Kraus: p. 108(tl).

Library of Congress: pp. 135(cl), 136(t).

NASA (National Aeronautics and Space Administration): pp. 14(t,bl), 28(tl), 50, 72, 91(cr,bc), 208.

Nature Picture Library: pp. 10(t), 78(br), 84, 128(t), 178(cr), 206(t).

pngkey: p. 150(hearts).

Science Photo Library: pp. 58, 96(br).

Wikimedia Commons: pp. 6, 40, 135(cr), 181(cr), 182(cr).

Credits

Text and cover design copyright © 2022 by
Penguin Random House LLC

All rights reserved. Published in the United States by Bright Matter
Books, an imprint of Random House Children's Books, a division of
Penguin Random House LLC, New York.

Bright Matter Books and the colophon are registered trademarks of
Penguin Random House LLC.

Visit us on the Web! **rhcbooks.com**

Educators and librarians, for a variety of teaching tools, visit us
at **RHTeachersLibrarians.com**

Library of Congress Cataloging-in-Publication Data is available
upon request.
ISBN 978-0-593-51640-9 (trade)
ISBN 978-0-593-51641-6 (lib. bdg.)
ISBN 978-0-593-51642-3 (ebook)

COVER PHOTO CREDITS:
Front Cover Photos: Shutterstock/M.Aurelius(Astronaunt)
                        Shutterstock/Jurik Peter(Mars)
Back Cover Photo: Dreamstime.

MANUFACTURED IN ITALY
10 9 8 7 6 5 4 3 2 1
First Edition

Produced by Fun Factory Press, LLC, in association with
Potomac Global Media, LLC.

The publisher would like to thank the following people for their
contributions to this book: Melina Gerosa Bellows, President,
Fun Factory Press, and Series Creator and Author; Priyanka
Lamichhane, Editor and Project Manager; Chad Tomlinson, Art
Director; Heather McElwain, Copy Editor; Mary Stephanos, Fact-
checker; Potomac Global Media: Kevin Mulroy, Publisher; Barbara
Brownell Grogan, Editor in Chief; Christopher L. Mazzatenta,
Designer; Susannah Jayes and Ellen Dupont, Picture Researchers;
Jane Sunderland and Heather McElwain, Contributing Editors

TOTALLY RANDOM QUESTIONS
FOR TOTALLY COOL KIDS!